Technology 2015

Scott Tilley

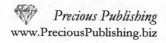

Precious Publishing
www.PreciousPublishing.biz

ISBN: 1503227669
ISBN-13: 978-1503227668

TABLE OF CONTENTS

DEDICATION

This book is dedicated to the computer science and software engineering students at the Florida Institute of Technology. Many of the columns in this book were discussed as part of the course, "CSE 3030: Legal, Ethical, and Social Issues of Computing" during Fall 2013. I particularly enjoyed hearing the younger generations' views on the subject of privacy in the Internet age.

PREFACE

This is a complete collection of my Technology Today columns from 2013. The column appears each week in the business section of the *Florida Today* (Gannett) newspaper. The newspaper primarily serves Brevard County and the Space Coast region of Florida's beautiful east coast.

The emergent theme of 2013 was **our connected world**, which was reflected in stories related to privacy (Edward Snowden and the NSA), complexity (HealthCare.gov), and fragility (vulnerable infrastructure and digital device dependency). It seems like a day didn't go by when one of these three topics was in the mainstream media. The speed of technological change just seems to be increasing, and with it the scope of technology's impact on every aspect of our lives.

As with previous volumes in this series, the columns included here are the unedited versions I submit to the newspaper. For each column I include my title, a subtitle that I include as a suggestion to the editors of what they might consider for print and online headlines, and the actual headline used. Any errors or omissions in the book are mine alone.

Many people have asked me where I get my ideas for the columns. My answer is simple: just look around – the modern world is full of technology-related stories. Being on a weekly deadline helps focus the mind too. ☺

As always, I hope you find this collection interesting. Please feel free to contact me anytime. I can be reached via email at TechnologyToday@srtilley.com, you can follow my column @TechTodayColumn on Twitter, and you can find me on Facebook.

Scott Tilley

Melbourne, FL

Calendar for year 2013 (United States)

January
S	M	T	W	T	F	S
	1	2	3	4	5
6	7	8	9	10	11	12
13	14	15	16	17	18	19
20	21	22	23	24	25	26
27	28	29	30	31

◑:4 ●:11 ◐:18 ○:26

February
S	M	T	W	T	F	S
					1	2
3	4	5	6	7	8	9
10	11	12	13	14	15	16
17	18	19	20	21	22	23
24	25	26	27	28

◑:3 ●:10 ◐:17 ○:25

March
S	M	T	W	T	F	S
					1	2
3	4	5	6	7	8	9
10	11	12	13	14	15	16
17	18	19	20	21	22	23
24	25	26	27	28	29	30
31

◑:4 ●:11 ◐:19 ○:27

April
S	M	T	W	T	F	S
	1	2	3	4	5	6
7	8	9	10	11	12	13
14	15	16	17	18	19	20
21	22	23	24	25	26	27
28	29	30

◑:3 ●:10 ◐:18 ○:25

May
S	M	T	W	T	F	S
			1	2	3	4
5	6	7	8	9	10	11
12	13	14	15	16	17	18
19	20	21	22	23	24	25
26	27	28	29	30	31

◑:2 ●:9 ◐:18 ○:25 ◑:31

June
S	M	T	W	T	F	S
						1
2	3	4	5	6	7	8
9	10	11	12	13	14	15
16	17	18	19	20	21	22
23	24	25	26	27	28	29
30

●:8 ◐:16 ○:23 ◑:30

July
S	M	T	W	T	F	S
	1	2	3	4	5	6
7	8	9	10	11	12	13
14	15	16	17	18	19	20
21	22	23	24	25	26	27
28	29	30	31

●:8 ◐:15 ○:22 ◑:29

August
S	M	T	W	T	F	S
				1	2	3
4	5	6	7	8	9	10
11	12	13	14	15	16	17
18	19	20	21	22	23	24
25	26	27	28	29	30	31

●:6 ◐:14 ○:20 ◑:28

September
S	M	T	W	T	F	S
1	2	3	4	5	6	7
8	9	10	11	12	13	14
15	16	17	18	19	20	21
22	23	24	25	26	27	28
29	30

●:5 ◐:12 ○:19 ◑:26

October
S	M	T	W	T	F	S
		1	2	3	4	5
6	7	8	9	10	11	12
13	14	15	16	17	18	19
20	21	22	23	24	25	26
27	28	29	30	31

●:4 ◐:11 ○:18 ◑:26

November
S	M	T	W	T	F	S
					1	2
3	4	5	6	7	8	9
10	11	12	13	14	15	16
17	18	19	20	21	22	23
24	25	26	27	28	29	30

●:3 ◐:10 ○:17 ◑:25

December
S	M	T	W	T	F	S
1	2	3	4	5	6	7
8	9	10	11	12	13	14
15	16	17	18	19	20	21
22	23	24	25	26	27	28
29	30	31

●:2 ◐:9 ○:17 ◑:25

Jan 1	New Year's Day	May 27	Memorial Day	Nov 11	Veterans Day
Jan 21	Martin Luther King Day	Jun 16	Fathers' Day	Nov 28	Thanksgiving Day
Feb 14	Valentine's Day	Jul 4	Independence Day	Dec 24	Christmas Eve
Feb 18	Presidents' Day	Sep 2	Labor Day	Dec 25	Christmas Day
Mar 31	Easter Sunday	Oct 14	Columbus Day	Dec 31	New Year's Eve
May 12	Mothers' Day	Oct 31	Halloween		

CES 2013

For the first time in 15 years, no keynote from Microsoft

Published as "What to expect from the Consumer Electronics Show"

January 4, 2013 (418 words)

The giant Consumer Electronics Show (CES) takes place next week in Las Vegas. It's a huge event. Last year there were over 156,000 attendees. What new and exciting developments can we expect in 2013?

Ultra HD TV: Just when you thought your new flat-panel television was state-of-the-art, along comes a new standard that promises even higher clarity that regular High Definition (HD) pictures. Ultra HD is also known as 4K. It increases the screen resolution from 1920x1080 (HD) to 3840x2160 pixels. The movie "The Hobbit" was shot in 4K (and at 48 frames per second, double the usual 24fps), but personally I couldn't see much difference when I saw it in the theater.

Verdict: Skip it. Like 3D TV, this is mostly a gimmick by manufacturers to get you to upgrade.

Smartphones: Everyone but Apple will have new smartphones on display at CES. Most will be Android devices with little new functionality but more of the same: larger screens, faster processors, better cameras. I don't relish the idea of carrying a phone the size of an iPad Mini in my pocket, and I don't need a quad-core processor to make a call.

Verdict: Wait for the iPhone 5S (or the iPhone 6). The dark horse in this race is RIM's BlackBerry 10, which is due to be released at the end of January.

Tablets: Many of the same companies pushing their smartphones are

1

pushing their Android-branded tablets. There's very little to distinguish tablets these days beyond size and price. But tablets are definitely outpacing conventional PCs, even in the enterprise.

Verdict: Apple is rumored to be releasing another upgrade to the iPad in March. Other than Amazon.com's Kindle Fire HD and Barnes & Noble's Nook, there's too much churn in the market for other tablets to make much of an impact.

Microsoft: For the first time in 15 years, Microsoft is not giving a keynote at CES. It will be a bit weird not to see Bill Gates or Steve Ballmer striding the stage, offering their perspective on the technology landscape. But there's not too much new for them to say in 2013. Last year Ballmer focused on the Metro interface used in Windows Phones and Windows 8. Their Xbox continues to sell well, but there's nothing really new with the platform.

Verdict: It's unclear who will claim the mantle of technology leader for CES. Apple and Google could, but neither seems willing to do so. For now it's the chipmakers and the media companies taking the spotlight.

NEST

A next-generation online thermostat that programs itself

Published as "Next-generation online thermostat programs itself then learns about you"

January 11, 2013 (436 words)

One of the themes at this year's Consumer Electronics Show in Las Vegas is "connected devices". It seems everything is on the Internet now, from the proverbial fridge and coffee maker to watches, TVs, even cutlery. Usually having a household appliance become computerized and put online just leads to unnecessary complexity, but sometimes it can make life easier.

I've been using a fascinating new thermostat called "The Nest" since last November. It's Wi-Fi enabled so you can manage the device with an Internet connection. It even has a smartphone app that lets you control the device while you're on the road.

It sounds complicated, but it's actually very simple. I've always avoided programmable thermostats because the interface was terrible, batteries wore out, and installation was problematic. The Nest has none of these negatives.

You don't program the Nest (although you can). Instead, it learns what you want. Each day it tracks the settings at different times of the day. After a week or so it has "learned" your favorite temperature settings.

At $249, the Nest is expensive, but does save money. In fact, this week I received the latest "Nest Energy Report" detailing usage in my home for December 2012. The report shows how often the air conditioner ran for the month, the kWh used, how many "Leafs" I earned, and so on. A "Leaf" is earned when the Nest uses an energy-efficient temperature setting; a small green leaf appears on the display. In my case, this appears most often during the day, when the Nest automatically detects that you're away from home and shifts the temperature settings accordingly.

There's also a certain coolness factor that comes from having such an elegant device hanging on your wall. Ex-Apple people founded Nest, and their design and engineering expertise shows. The controls couldn't be simpler. You just turn the solid metal ring on the outside of the Nest to turn the temperature up or down. Pushing the center display, which acts like a large button, accesses other functions.

Setup was easy and installation was idiot-proof, although not apparently meeting the higher standard of "Scott proof", since I managed to misconnect one wire. However, the Nest detected the fault and the problem was quickly resolved. Nest customer service is great too: they follow up by personal email and they even had real people answering the phone.

For our neighbors up north, the Nest probably makes even more sense. I have a friend who just spent $600 for one month of heating oil. If a thermostat can help lower your bills for a few months, it will pay for itself.

JAVA

Just say 'No'

Published as "Security flaws continue to plague Java"

January 18, 2013 (436 words)

I told you so.

Don't say I didn't warn you, because I did. Last November, I wrote an article outlining some of the many flaws of the Java programming language and runtime environment. I ended the article by saying, "Java needs to be eradicated."

The feedback I received from that Java column was ... passionate, shall we say. Several people asked how I could be so negative on Java, since it was "clearly a success." Others wondered about my intentions, my background, even my biological history.

This week, Java is in the news again, for all the wrong reasons. A zero-day exploit was found in the latest release of Java, Version 7 Update 10. Carnegie Mellon University's CERT put out a security alert with technical details of the flaw, "[a] vulnerability that can allow a remote, unauthenticated attacker to execute arbitrary code on a vulnerable system." It's called a "zero day" attack because the exploit is known and already being used by hackers, but the flaw has not yet been fixed.

Hackers don't even need to understand how the security vulnerability works. So-called "script kiddies" can buy the attack as part of exploit kits that are sold online. The exploit is as simple as redirecting someone to a website that has the malicious Java code on it. If Java is enabled in your browser, the code runs and the hackers have control of your machine, your data, anything they want.

This security problem with Java is so serious that the US Department of Homeland Security (DHS) even issued a warning to the general public. I can't remember the last time this was done for a programming language.

The DHS recommended that all users disable Java software on their computers to avoid being hacked.

Oracle has issued a partial fix for the attack, but the fix is not complete, so the attack can still take place. And it requires users to update Java on all their computers – which we all know is never easy. For example, CERT's advisory states, "Due to what appears to potentially be a bug in the Java installer, the Java Control Panel applet may be missing on some Windows systems." It would be laughable if it were not so serious. It's like the Keystone Cops are in charge of Java.

At some point, we as computer users will say, "enough is enough" to these constant security flaws in commonly used applications. We'd never put up with such incompetence in other aspects of our lives, like car manufacturing or medicine.

Follow Nancy Reagan's advice when it comes to drugs or Java: "Just say no."

TEXT-TO-SPEECH

A great way to use technology to help improve your writing

Published as "Does this sound right? Now, you can know"

January 25, 2013 (410 words)

A common use of computer technology is voice recognition. You speak to a computer and it translates your speech into a format it can understand. It's the reason those annoying automated phone "help" systems can exist.

I choose to use a more helpful variation of this technology: text-to-speech. Instead of turning what I say into words, I turn what I write into audio. I've found it an invaluable aid in editing drafts of my musings.

It's well known that we all learn in different modes: visual, aural, touch, and so on. We can also detect when something doesn't seem right by leverage these different modes of interaction. I often tell my computer science students that buggy programs can be fixed using their Aunt Agatha. It works like this: Instead of staring at a screen for hours at a time, you verbally describe your problem to your aunt. She doesn't need to understand anything that you're saying for her to help. Just the act of verbalizing your conundrum makes you think about it differently. Some schools use stuffed animals in place of real people to speak to – it works just as effectively.

Having your writing read aloud to you has a similar effect. Instead of thinking about the text, re-reading the same words many times, you can hear how your writing sounds to the reader (listener). This simple change of communication medium brings errors to the surface. It makes awkward sentences obvious. It can really help with the editing process by eliminating the need to manually fix simple syntax issues.

The best way to have your work read aloud is to have an actual person do it – your own Aunt Agatha. But if no one is available, your computer can help. There are several text-to-speech programs available that will read your words back to you. I use the built-in program that comes with the Mac. I can adjust the voice (male/female, accent, pitch, tone, and speed) so that the written words sound the most understandable to my ear. I just select the text I want to hear and the computer translates the words into sounds.

I've been using this technique for nearly 30 years. I've found it an invaluable aid as an automated copy-editing service. It's a simple but effective use of technology to help improve your writing.

Hmm ... maybe I should have ran this column through the text-to-speech engine before I submitted it. Too busy I guess. Next time!

FITBIT

How a little bit of technology can help with exercise and fitness

Published as "Fitbit: A bit of technology helps with fitness"

February 1, 2013 (428 words)

This Sunday is the Melbourne Music Marathon. Anything with the word "marathon" in it scares me; it sounds like way too much work.

Fortunately for those of us who are more "exercise challenged," there are the Florida Today 5K & 8K events on Saturday. Since I'm more of a sloth than a cheetah, I'm planning on a relaxed 5K shuffle.

To help me get in shape, I've turned to – what else – technology. I've been using a very popular little gadget called the "Fitbit One" to track my daily activities. It's one of many new personal health-monitoring devices that have been introduced in the last few years.

The Fitbit is about the size of an AA battery. It comes with a small rubber cover you can use to clip the Fitbit to your belt or shirt. I just carry the Fitbit in my pocket.

The Fitbit has a simple user interface with one button that you push to change the tiny display to show your progress throughout the day. The Fitbit silently records your daily activities: steps taken, floors climbed, miles traveled, and calories burned. It magically resets itself at midnight.

There is a very good smartphone app for the Fitbit too. The phone communicates with the device via Bluetooth. The program syncs data from the Fitbit and pushes it to the cloud, so that you can access your account on the web.

Using the smartphone app or the Fitbit website, you can log all the food you ate during the day. The program knows many common foods and converts them to calories, fat, and so on automatically. (Rather like your body does.) If you record your weight, the Fitbit can adjust its estimates of calories burned accordingly.

The Fitbit can also be used to monitor your sleep patterns. You put it in a small wristband and it senses when you fall asleep and how many times you wake during the night. The latter is valuable information for those with shallow sleep patterns.

Fitbit also lets you share your results with family and friends, rather like an exercise-oriented social network. You can use the connections for encouragement. The Fitbit itself gives you messages when you near your targets, such as "Almost there!" when you get close to your daily step goal.

Believe me, if this device can motivate a slug like to move a bit more each day, it can motivate anyone. We'll see on Saturday if using the Fitbit has helped me with my 5K stroll. But to be honest, I'm mostly looking forward to the post-race pizza.

VALENTINE'S DAY

Ditch the technology and focus on the wetware

Published as "Declare Valentine's your no-keyboard day"

February 8, 2013 (430 words)

There are many "Valentine's Day Tech Gift Guides" available online. Rather than give you my opinion on the latest gadget to woo your Valentine's (Wi-Fi enabled waffle maker anyone?), I thought I'd suggest a different approach to making this Valentine's Day special: ditch the technology.

You read the right. The technology guy is telling you to stop using technology. At least for one day, try to minimize your use of it. Focus instead on your Valentine. Who knows, you might be richly rewarded for your personal attention.

Here are a few do's and don'ts for a successful and technology-free Valentine's Day:

DO speak to your Valentine. And by "speak" I mean talk, not type. In person. Face to face. With no distractions. I understand that sometimes distance makes real dates impossible, in which case you'll have to settle for a shared experience with Skype.

DO NOT check Facebook, send text messages, browse the web, do email, or chat online while at dinner. Remember what the flight attendants tell you to do on an airplane: if it's got an on/off switch, turn it off. It's amazing to me how many people stare at their smart phones at dinner, even while eating, instead of paying attention to the person they're with. Not only is it impolite, it's not very romantic either. Social networks only provide artificial social interactions. Focus instead on the real social interaction right in front of you.

DO give your Valentine's a card. A real one. Printed, on paper, in an envelope. The kind where you can write a personal message inside – with a pen, in your own hand. It's old school, but it works. There's a reason Hallmark is still in business after all these years.

DO NOT give your Valentine a lame techno-gift. Catalogs from places like Brookstone are full of cool-looking items. Once you see them, you want them. Indeed, you wonder how you lived without one for all this time. You feel this way because the advertisement creates a false sense of need. Does your honey really need electric shoelaces or Bluetooth-enabled towel dryers or automatic watch winders? No. What they need is something that reflects your personality and conveys your feelings towards them.

DO dress up and go out. There is value in formality, and putting on nice clothes for a special restaurant lends Valentine's Day a certain gravitas. For you geeks, iPhone holsters are the modern-day equivalent of pocket protectors: lose them. Above all, don't wear those dorky Bluetooth earpieces with the blinking blue lights – you'll look like a cyborg on a date.

ENGINEERS WEEK

How tinkering with hardware sparked my interest in engineering

Published as "Young engineers must tinker with stuff"

February 15, 2013 (432 words)

There is a small neon light that has been burning brightly in my basement for over 30 years. Every time I go downstairs I'm greeted with a familiar orange glow. The tiny light is inside a push button switch; when pressed, the overhead light goes on, illuminating my old workbench.

The workbench is really a salvaged kitchen table. It's cluttered with assorted tools, debris from recent projects, and detritus from old ones. Above the workbench is a pegboard that holds odds and ends like loops of wire and rolls of electrical tape. To the right of the workbench are several wall-mounted storage cabinets, each drawer carefully labeled to indicate its contents: resistors, capacitors, switches, transistors and integrated circuits, and so on. Many of the parts on the workbench and in the cabinets are so old that they give the basement a certain aroma, like burned solder and ozone.

I work with software for a living, but my interest in engineering began with hardware. The workbench was my playground and old TVs were my toys. I enjoyed taking them apart, sorting the tubes and transistors, seeing how they worked. Later I worked part-time doing TV repair, earning some pocket money during my high school and early college days.

I didn't start with TVs of course. When I was very young I spent hours creating elaborate mechanical devices like construction cranes with my Meccano set. Later I learned about electronics using kits that you can still buy at places like Radio Shack. The kits provide an experiment platform for young hobbyists to explore the fascinating workings of diodes, circuits, and chips. I built simple things like digital clocks, light chasers and strobe lights, and stereo amplifiers.

When I was more adventurous I tried to build "worm turners" for fishing. This required me to first build an arc lamp using a glass bowl full of salt water, lead sinkers, and two battery cores wired to the mains. I blew a few fuses, but the arc was amazing to see. I could melt nails in the inferno it produced.

Next week is Engineers Week. It's a good opportunity to think about all the great things in our modern world that were made possible by engineers (and not just arc welders). It's also a great time to get young people interested in engineering. If they don't like mechanics or electronics, try a chemistry set, or a model plane, or a radio-controlled boat. There's something for everyone. But most importantly, make the experience hands-on, tactile, and real. There's plenty of time for the artificial world of software later.

CYBER ATTACKS

Modern espionage with a "license to hack"

Published as "Don't let cyber attacks happen to you"

February 22, 2013 (434 words)

Ian Fleming's original novels about the spy James Bond included a character called 'Q' (Quartermaster) who was responsible for providing all the neat gadgets that Bond used in the field. If Fleming was writing today he might introduce a new character called 'C' (Cyber) or 'H' (Hacker) who worked in Q Branch. Given recent real-world events, it seems computer security has become synonymous with modern espionage.

By now most people are aware of media reports concerning numerous cyber attacks on large companies, government agencies, and infrastructure control centers (e.g., the power grid). Security firms such as Mandiant say the attacks have been traced back to one or more units within the Chinese army. They've even identified the nondescript office building on the outskirts of Shanghai that they claim houses the hackers.

The Chinese don't have an exclusive "license to hack" of course. Other attacks against Western entities have been traced to many other places, including Russia, Eastern Europe, and former Soviet republics. The US Government itself uses cyber attacks as part of its overall defense strategy, as witnessed by the Stuxnet and Flame worms successfully used with the help of Israel against the Iranian nuclear program.

Some cyber attacks are made possible by inherent flaws in commonly used applications. For example, the serious flaw in the Java applet plug-in for Web browsers that I wrote about a few weeks ago was the probable source of recent security breaches in in companies such as Apple, Facebook, and Twitter. Other cyber attacks are far more sophisticated, often going undetected (or unreported) for months at a time.

It's amazing how little infrastructure is needed to wreak such

15

international havoc. Hackers don't need "boots on the ground," they use "bits on the network" to do their dirty work. They even employ computers owned by unsuspecting users in coordinated attacks on multiple targets. These computers are known as "zombies" and like their horror movie inspirations they are hard to kill.

Computer security companies like MacAfee and Symantec are playing catch-up now, and that's not good. The new attacks are extremely difficult to detect using traditional anti-virus technology. Security patches always follow security holes; we should be doing better engineering to avoid the holes in the first place.

How could these cyber attacks affect you? Perhaps the biggest threat to individual users are called "phishing attacks," which involve tricking you into opening email attachment or clicking on links that you think are legitimate, but in fact send you to websites infected with malware that infects your computer – often without you even knowing it's happened. Don't let it happen to you.

NOOK

Digital content trumps digital devices for Barnes & Noble

Published as "Nook simply couldn't cut it in e-reader competition"

March 1, 2013 (437 words)

In November 2011 the Canadian bookstore Indigo sold their Kobo e-book reader to a Japanese company for $315 million. Indigo operates the largest chain of bookstores in Canada, under several brands including Chapters and Coles. But even their size relative to the Canadian market was no match for the major players such as Amazon.com and Apple.

A year and a half later, it seems like Barnes & Noble may be following a similar path by selling (or discontinuing) their Nook e-book reader. This would mark a significant change of direction for the company. For the last few years they've had a major push on their branded e-book reader. It is given prominent display space at the front of the store. You literally can't miss it.

Unfortunately for Barnes & Noble, the competition for e-book readers has gotten even fiercer recently, with tablets powered by Google's Android operating system entering the fray. While sales of digital media and e-books have increased, the Nook has not been the device of choice for most consumers. The iPad and the Kindle still rule.

For traditionalists like myself, I prefer reading real books. But there are some types of content that I enjoy on a dedicated e-book reader, such as newspapers and text-oriented magazines. I still use the second-generation Kindle everyday. I've tried the newer models, including the touchscreen Kindle and the Kindle Fire, but I did not like the interface as much as the simple controls on the older Kindle.

I felt the same when using the iPad or the iPad Mini to read newspapers. Like the Kindle Fire, the iPad is an excellent device for multimedia content like music or movies, and for magazines with lots of graphics and embedded audio or video. But for straight text, I found the passive electronic ink display of the Kindle superior to the active screens on the Fire or the iPad.

The truth is that content is king. The device is just a delivery vehicle, and it changes all the time. Amazon.com knows this, which is why they also offer their e-book reader as an app on most platforms. Their goal is to sell you the book, not the reader. Perhaps Barnes & Noble is coming to the same conclusion.

For us consumers, one less e-book reader on the market won't make that much of a difference. But without the Nook available the future of Barnes & Noble becomes a bit more uncertain. Personally I hope they stick around for a long time. After all, they are the last major bricks-and-mortar bookstore around, and I'd hate to see them disappear from our communities.

WORKING FROM HOME

Yahoo!'s Marissa Mayer channels Ebenezer Scrooge at work

Published as "Yahoo! leader could find herself very alone"

March 8, 2013 (438 words)

A few years ago I had a funded research project with a large German automotive company. The company placed one of their senior engineers in my lab at the university for a year. Near the start of the project it quickly became apparent we had to address a cultural issue related to working arrangements and attendance expectations. The engineer became concerned when graduate students working on the project were not at their desks promptly at 8:00am. His normal working environment was a traditional 8:00am – 5:00pm schedule at the office. He couldn't see how we could get work done with people coming and going at all hours. But that's the way things are in a research environment. Once he came to terms with this new reality, he adjusted very well. The project was a success.

It's too bad that Yahoo!'s CEO Marissa Mayer was not part of that project, because then she may have learned how knowledge workers excel when given the freedom to innovate. One aspect of that freedom is the choice of where and when to work. As long as the job gets done properly, the rest should be immaterial.

For a company struggling to regain its leadership position under its sixth CEO in as many years, one would think that Yahoo!'s focus would be on innovation and growth. Instead, it appears their management has chosen to focus its attention on introducing 19th century work practices to Silicon Valley.

It won't work. No software engineer wants to be treated like Bob Cratchit.

One of the reasons stated for disallowing remote work is that it doesn't permit collaboration through serendipitous interaction. But such interactions can happen anytime now, not just in the office hallways – that's what technology is for. Chat rooms are used all the time to send quick questions to colleagues. Skype and other video conferencing programs can connect entire meetings online.

Good employees have a strong work ethic: they work everywhere (coffee shops, on the bus and train, in the airports) and all the time (during the day, in the evening, and on weekends). In exchange, they expect to be treated as responsible adults. They do not respond well to old-style work regulations that make little sense today.

It's true that there will always be people who abuse the system. But this reflects a lack of leadership and shared vision. Curtailing workplace freedoms is not the answer. The valuable people will leave; the Wally's will stay, punching the digital clock.

The time of measuring productivity by how long an employee sits in a cubicle is long gone. If Yahoo! doesn't reverse course, they will be too.

BIRTHDAY WISHES

Blow out the virtual candles and make wishes come true

Published as "Happy Day! Stop texting so much, already"

March 15, 2013 (424 words)

Today is my birthday. It's traditional to be granted a wish (or two) when you blow out the candles. I've already done that using my iPhone app that let's me blow out virtual candles. Really!

Usually birthday wishes are kept secret, but just this once I'll share a few of technology-related ones (in no particular order). Maybe by sharing them a few will come true.

I wish people would stop using social media as a replacement for real interaction. At home and at work, people are choosing gadgets over people. Why go out to dinner if you're going to spend the entire time looking at your phone? Why not call someone (or better yet, walk to their office) instead of sending them email?

At school, every time I enter a classroom the students are sitting, heads down, playing with their smartphones. It's as quiet as a library – and about as close to a real library that most current students will ever get. Where's the pre-class chitchat?

I wish technology would be a lot easier to use. The root cause of many of the problems associated with computers and technology in general is complexity. We've created devices that have incomprehensible interfaces, written by geeks who seem to have no knowledge of usability design. There's one proven way to change this: stop buying shoddy products and the market will respond.

I wish we'd find a way to reduce the risks associated with cybersecurity. These risks span the gamut from personal to international. I'm concerned that this year and the next will see a dramatic increase in security exploits targeting mobile devices. Think of all the important information you carry on your phone. Now think of that information being stolen without you even knowing it was taken.

Cyberattacks have become a national security issue. It's not too far fetched to imagine a real war breaking out due to damage caused by a cyberwar. It's like the Wild West in cyberspace these days. Where is the cyber-Cavalry?

I wish more young people would see the value of a career in science, technology, engineering, or mathematics (STEM). Our nation needs an educated and savvy workforce. Not everyone can (or should) grow up to be Justin Bieber; a few more Bill Gates and Steve Jobs would be fine too.

I wish we'd drop daylight savings time. We don't have an energy crisis. Most of us don't live agrarian lifestyles on a farm. Pardon the pun, but who's got time to adjust all those clocks? I've got birthday celebrations to enjoy!

iPHONE BANKING

Why waste time going to the ATM when there's an app for that?

Published as "Smartphones help technology skip a step"

March 22, 2013 (420 words)

While most of America was being crisscrossed with copper wire for landlines, many people in the developing world remained disconnected from the outside world. Until now.

In places like Africa and Asia, many countries completely bypassed the landline telephone era and went straight to cell phones. Now cell phones are so ubiquitous that the technology has helped the countries leapfrog others in several ways. For example, people use their cell phones to buy transit tickets, to shop at local vendors, even to pay their bills. The costs are added to their cell phone bill. Simple and efficient.

We're not there yet. But a few new smartphone apps that are now available are helping us catch up. Banking is one good example where technology has made some tedious tasks obsolete – like depositing a cheque.

While at lunch recently, a friend mentioned how frustrated she was with limited banking hours. She wanted to deposit a cheque but always did it in person at the branch. With the bank closed, she couldn't deposit her cheque. She'd never used the ATM for anything other than the occasional cash withdrawal, and in today's increasingly cashless society, even those transactions were few and far between.

My first thought was to tell her to use the ATM, which are open 24/7. Most banks introduced "envelope-less deposits" at their ATMs within the last two years. The ATM scans each cheque directly. The system still has problems with cheques that have fancy watermarks and mixed colors, but generally it works well.

However, why waste time driving to the bank to use the ATM when you have an app on your smartphone that can save you the trip?

The major banks now allow you to deposit your cheque simply by taking a picture of it with your phone. The app takes care of everything else. This means no more trips to the ATM; you can literally deposit cheques from anywhere now.

This feature is a great example of a technical solution to an old problem: what to do with physical cheques. Banks much prefer dealing with electronic transfers than with paper documents. The smartphone app solves this problem.

My friend downloaded the bank's app to her iPhone while in the coffee shop. She took a photo of the cheque placed on the table and received immediate confirmation of the deposit. She also got to keep the physical cheque for her records; the bank didn't need to mail it back to her.

She's skipped the ATM era entirely. Simple and efficient.

KEY FOBS

A solution in search of a problem

Published as "Key fobs: A solution in search of a problem"

March 29, 2013 (414 words)

The electronics industry continues to introduce solutions to problems that don't exist. Key fobs used in many cars these days are a prime example.

The first problem is the name: "fob". Only geeks could introduce such a weird word for something that already had a perfectly good name: key. True, a fob is more than a traditional key, but that's part of the problem.

Fobs were introduced as a more secure and convenient way to open your car doors and start the engine. Instead of inserting the key into the lock or the ignition, the fob merely needs to be close to car's control systems to work. Inside the fob is a small radio that communicates with a paired unit in the dashboard.

Keyless entry systems do have some value. When it's raining outside you don't need to fumble for the key to open the door; when you approach the car the doors automatically unlock. Unless of course the battery in the fob is dead, or the receiver in the car is not working, in which case you're stuck.

Keyless ignition systems seem less valuable. When you insert a real key and turn it to start the car, there's a certain physicality to it. Even more important, you know you have to turn off the engine to get your key out before exiting the car. With a fob, you can forget to turn off the car when you park. I know people who have walked away from their car, oblivious to the fact that it was still running – and unlocked.

Some fobs are sold as add-ons to reduce car theft. You need both the physical key and the fob to start the car – sort of a belt-and-suspenders approach. Unfortunately, these after-markets fobs are often less reliable than the built-in models. This can result in owners sitting in their driveway, cursing and waiving the fob around, while the engine just makes clicking noises. This happened to me with a friend's car when visiting up north. It was a frigid 16 degrees below zero and I was stuck outside because the darn fob was not working. It was too cold for it to function properly!

Automobiles and technology are now deeply intertwined, sometimes positively, sometimes not. For example, Google is working on cars that can drive themselves. Subaru appears to have a more modest goal: cars that can start themselves. Accidentally. This phenomenon has been reported as the "zombie car problem." The cause: a malfunctioning fob.

Eye Tracking Phones

Your life as seen through the camera eye

Published as "Soon, your phone might be watching you"

April 5, 2013 (412 words)

Do you want your phone to watch you? Pretty soon it will. Like it or not.

The phone won't just listen to you speak and understand what you say, like Apple's Siri. I mean it will literally watch you, your facial expressions, even your eye movements. Samsung must think you want this, which is why they've introduced this new feature in their latest Galaxy S4 smartphone.

Eye tracking technology is not new, but it's new in a phone. It's been used before for scientific experiments, for advanced heads-up displays in pilot helmets, and to help the severely disabled. Until now the hardware has been bulky and expensive, and the software has been problematic and inaccurate. However, advances in technology have now made it possible for even the limited capabilities of the camera in a phone to act as a passable eye tracking system.

The Galaxy S4 uses its new capabilities as more of a proof-of-concept than for anything truly useful. For example, when looking at a video playing on the device, when you move your eyes away from the screen the video pauses and restarts when you look at the screen again. But this is just the beginning of what could be a truly remarkable change in the way we interact with our phones. It represents the next generation of swipe gestures, but without physical touch, using your eyes instead of your fingers.

The commoditization of eye tracking hardware and software has uses beyond smartphones. It could be used in games, in medicine, and as an aid for those with motor control issues (e.g., Parkinson's disease). If Samsung and other manufacturers open up their phone's eye tracking with an interface to third-party apps, the possibilities are endless.

Eye tracking could also be used for more nefarious purposes. Security

27

firms could use eye tracking as an additional authentication mechanism, but it could also be used to gain insight into what you're doing on the screen – including what you're typing (like passwords). Never mind trying to hide windows when people walk past your computer or phone – the system will have already recorded exactly what you were looking at, when, and for how long.

Eye tracking would be a boon for advertisers. Where you look on the screen clearly indicates you've seen something of interest. Real-time monitoring of your eye movement would enable incredibly focused advertisement to be served up to you dynamically. It's all very "Minority Report" and it's coming sooner than you think.

GOOGLE GLASS

Who watches the watchers?

Published as "Google Glass: Who watches the watchers?"

April 12, 2013 (418 words)

The Samsung Galaxy S4 smartphone has the ability to watch you: your face, your expressions, even your eye movements. Advertisers may love it, but personally I find it a bit creepy. I don't want to be tracked like that.

But would I be OK tracking others? What if I had a device that looked outwards, like a second set of eyes? A device that could record everything I see and hear in real time, and even broadcast to the Internet for the whole world to follow? It could turn everyone's life into his or her very own Truman Show – the ultimate enabler for narcissistic reality TV shows.

If you think this is a good idea, say hello to Google Glass.

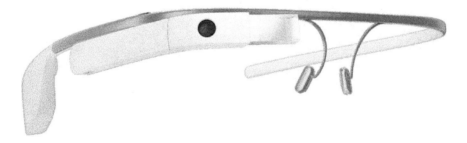

Google Glass is still in the prototype stage of development. But even Google's co-founder, Sergey Brin, was spotted wearing a pair on the New York City subway a few months ago. Think of Google Glass as the ultimate personal assistant. It responds to voice command and eye movement. You can search for things you are looking at. It provides a heads-up display like that used by Air Force fighter pilots, but with a pair of glasses that look quite similar to sunglasses, with a small addition to project images.

The broadcast aspect of Google Glass has not been explored as much as the personal assistant capabilities. I can imagine how having a map overlay what I'm looking at might help me while driving. I can also imagine how assistive capabilities will give teachers headaches in the classroom when exams are taken. It would be like students using a lifeline all the time.

Modern society has created legal mechanisms to enforce expectations of privacy. Rapid advances in technology like Google Glass are obviating these provisions. We need look no further than Steve Mann, a professor at the University of Toronto who has been exploring wearable computing and smart clothing for over 20 years. Early versions of his EyeTap glasses made him look like a cyborg, but the newest version looks a lot like Google Glass. Last summer Mann got in trouble when visiting a McDonald's restaurant in Paris while wearing his EyeTap glasses. Some people there did not like him recording their actions without their consent. An incident ensued and Mann left the restaurant, but his augmented glasses had recorded (and uploaded) the entire event.

The impact of Google Glass will be known in the next few years. But once Google Glass becomes Google Implant, all bets are off.

SENIOR DESIGN PROJECTS

Learn by doing

Published as "College seniors learn by doing design projects"

April 19, 2013 (411 words)

There is a saying in engineering education: "Learn by doing." It's a motto that's used at Carnegie Mellon University's Silicon Valley campus, reflecting the entrepreneurial focus of their graduate programs. It's also a pedagogical philosophy that I share.

All engineering is grounded in science, but it's the disciplined application of core principles that makes engineering such an exciting career. In my own classes I usually begin by discussing underlying theories, illustrated with real-world examples of how the theories can impact products and services used in our everyday lives. It's true that the theory can sometimes seem dry, but context (and promises of what's to come) help keep the students engaged.

Once the theory is covered, it's practice, practice, practice. The students learn how to use the theory they've studied in team-based projects. Sometimes the projects are of their own choosing; sometimes I select the topic. When the first or second iteration is complete, I introduce tools and automation into the process. This usually helps emphasize the importance of scale in large engineering endeavors.

At the Florida Institute of Technology, most engineering and science undergraduate students enroll in a yearlong senior design project. They work in small teams, under the guidance of a faculty member, developing innovative solutions to exemplary problems. The projects span a very broad range, from bio-medical devices to experimental rocket engines.

Facilitating software engineering course projects for undergraduate (and graduate) students is a challenging task. The instructor must carefully balance the (sometimes) conflicting goals of academic rigor and industrial relevance. Some of the fundamental characteristics of software engineering projects (e.g., team-based, large-scale, long-lived) are difficult to realize within the constraints of a university course in a single semester. This is particularly true when dealing with young students who may lack the real-world experience needed to appreciate some of the more subtle aspects of software engineering. Over a decade ago I created a series of workshops called SWECP to explore how educators and industry can work together to develop a more rewarding educational experience for all stakeholders involved.

Today at the Clemente Center on Florida Tech's Melbourne campus is the Northrop Grumman Engineering and Science Student Design Showcase. Awards are presented to best projects in several disciplines. The competition is made possible by a $1 million endowment from Northrop Grumman Corporation. The showcase runs from 10:00am to 3:00pm and is free and open to the public. Come see what the next generation of scientists and engineers are capable of!

SURVEILLANCE

A society without the expectation of privacy

Published as "Under surveillance? Don't expect privacy"

April 26, 2013 (409 words)

The British TV show "Spooks" (called "MI-5" here) often showed the government agents using powerful computers with sophisticated image processing software to identify suspects caught on camera. They could use screen shots from still photographs or video streams from live feeds. Obviously the show is fiction, but it's not too far away from technical reality.

It helps that London, where MI-5 is headquartered in Thames House, is blanketed with closed circuit TV (CCTV) cameras. In fact, London is arguably the most heavily spied-upon city in the world. Reports suggest there are over half a million cameras in the capitol alone. With so many CCTV cameras watching the streets, it's very likely you'd be recorded going about your daily activities several times a day.

Here at home we don't have the same level of public CCTV surveillance as they do in the UK in most of our cities. But as the tragedy in Boston illustrated, we do have a good number of private CCTV cameras. We also have thousands of citizens who snap photos and videos on their phones all the time. When put together, these images do a reasonable job of recreating scenes where events took place.

Capturing criminals and terrorists using CCTV footage is obviously a good thing. But there's a dark side to the ubiquity of surveillance equipment in modern society: there's no longer an expectation of privacy. If you're out in public, you should assume you're being recorded. When Google Glass becomes commonplace, everyone will be recording everyone else – and uploading the results for the entire world to see, in real time. We may introduce legislation to disallow this sort of surreptitious recording, but for now technology is outpacing the legal system. It's also outpacing societal norms for ethical behavior. We just don't know what's appropriate in cyberspace.

Government agencies can provide any number of assurances that your actions, as tracked by CCTV, will not be used by anyone other than the property authorities. But you don't need to be paranoid to distrust these promises. Social engineering, hacking, and simple mistakes can create security vulnerabilities in any system, no matter what the original intention.

If George Orwell could see us now, he might wonder why we're so glad to accept such restrictions on our civil liberties. We're voluntarily moving towards a Big Brother society. It's no wonder that spy stores still do such brisk business. If you're going to be watched, why not return the favor?

TEACHERS

Take the time to thank the teachers in your life

Published as "At this time of year, don't forget to thank teachers"

May 3, 2013 (422 words)

This weekend is commencement at Florida Tech. Graduating students will be celebrating their academic accomplishments with friends and family. I hope they also take the time to thank the teachers who helped shape their lives.

Much has been written about the role of technology is education. It makes distance learning and online classes possible. It makes lab work and experiments more realistic. It makes research easier by bringing the world to our fingertips through computers and the web. But technology can never take the place of a good teacher.

Teachers profoundly affect students' lives. Growing up you often spend more time with your teacher in school than you do with your parents at home. At different stages of your studies, from elementary school to university, teachers influence how students think, how they act, and how they approach life's challenges.

I've been fortunate to have several teachers that I know positively impacted my own life and subsequent career. In Grade 6, Mr. Keuper instilled in me a lifelong love of reading and literature. He carefully read aloud an entire book to the class, one chapter a week, taking the whole school year. I can still hear his deep voice, filled with delight as he told the story to his rapt (and silent) audience. I spent the summer reading the next four books in the series.

My fascination with technology began in Grade 9 in Mr, Louvaris' Electronics class. I started like an apprentice electrician, wiring lights and switches in model homes in the lab. By Grade 11 I was repairing stereos and TVs. I loved the class so much I used to get special notes excusing myself from other courses so that I could spend more time on the bench. Mr, Louvaris let us stay late after school, working on special projects until dinnertime. I parlayed my experience in his class into summer jobs doing TV repair work that helped pay for my subsequent university studies.

Professor Müller had the biggest influence of any teacher on my life. He was my MSc advisor and my PhD supervisor. He was my mentor throughout my graduate studies and my early academic career. I've known him for over 25 years and I'm proud to call him a colleague and a friend.

Teachers mold you in ways you aren't always aware of at the time. A good teacher is a great model for all students. So take the time to thank one of your own teachers, past or present. They'll appreciate knowing that they made a difference.

SAAS

Why buy when you can rent?

Published as "Why buy software when you can rent?"

May 10, 2013 (425 words)

The average consumer does not have a power plant in their back yard. When they need electricity, they just plug the appliance into a wall socket and the juice flows. We pay FPL handsomely for this service, but we're only billed for as much power as we use.

The days of drawing water from a well are long gone for most of us too. I doubt many people would give up the convenience of indoor plumbing for a bucket and a rope. When we want drinkable water or a hot shower, we just turn on the tap. We pay the water company based on how much water we use and they take care of the rest.

Pretty soon we'll be treating software as a service (SaaS) too. Most people think of software as a product, something you buy in a box at the store. It comes on a disc that you install and maintain on your own computer. A few years ago some companies stopped making physical media; you had to download a digital copy from their website. But a real disc or a digital copy is still a product. You pay for it once, you download upgrades and patches every once in a while, and then you pay again when a new version is released.

The advent of cloud computing is changing all that. Instead of owning a copy of the software that you install on your own machine, you rent the software that is hosted on a remote server. It's not a product anymore – it's a service. You may pay a recurring fee each month, rather like a newspaper subscription. Or you may pay a variable fee based on how much computing resources (e.g., processor, storage) that you use, rather like your electricity and water services.

IBM was one of the first big companies to espouse this model of enterprise software as a service. Now many consumer-oriented companies are following along. For example, Adobe recently announced that their line of creative software programs will only be sold as online services. This means Photoshop won't be shipped in boxes or downloaded as images anymore. Instead, you'll subscribe to their "Creative Cloud" suite of services.

It may take a while to get used to leasing software as a service rather than owning the product, but in fact you never owned the software – you just purchased a temporary (and revocable) license. And you had to keep the software updated yourself. As the saying goes, "Why buy the cow when you can get the milk for free?"

CLONES

Send in the clones

Published as "Cloning people is bound to happen"

May 17, 2013 (424 words)

Should we clone people?

Note that I didn't prefix the question with, "If we could, ", because sooner or later we'll be able to do so. It's a question of when, not if. And given the rapid changes in both the science and engineering of cloning, that time may be here faster than you think.

Clones have been the stuff of science fiction for decades. For example, the replicants in the movie "Blade Runner" were advanced clones, nearly indistinguishable from humans. Their creators had genetically programmed the replicants to a shortened lifespan, which led to their rebellion.

Ironically, the movie was based on the 1968 book, "Do Androids Dream of Electric Sheep?" by Philip K. Dick. Nearly 30 years later, sheep were in the news again when science fiction became science fact with the cloning of Dolly the sheep in Scotland in 1996. Dolly gave birth several times and lived a relatively normal life. From all outward appearances, she was a typical sheep.

This week there were reports of scientists producing embryonic stem cells from cloned embryos. The embryos were created by inserting skin cells into donated eggs. Because stem cells can become any type of cell as they develop, some of the stem cells became heart cells, the first step in regenerating entire organs that are genetically equivalent to the cells cloned from the patient.

Bioethicists are concerned that this technique could ultimately be used to mature cloned embryos in surrogate mothers, leading to cloned humans. Medical researchers repeatedly say that this won't happen, that the technology is not mature enough, that it's unethical, and so on. But if it's possible, someone somewhere will do it. When it happens, the debate will quickly move from science and engineering to societal, philosophical, and even spiritual.

Spoiler alert! If you haven't seen "Oblivion," the new sci-fi movie with Tom Cruise, and you don't want to know about one of the major plot points in advance, stop reading this column now.

At the end of the movie, Tom Cruise's character finds out that he's a clone. There are many copies of himself running around a destroyed planet. They share some memories of the past but not their recent experiences. Nevertheless, one of the clones kills himself to save humanity from the machines who have conquered the Earth. He does so knowing that one of his clones will pick up his (their?) life back on the planet below.

This leads to a fundamental question that I'll leave to others to answer: What makes a person a person?

SUMMER READING

Sunscreen? Check. Beach chair? Check. Book? Check.

Published as "Keep tech in mind, on summer reading list"

May 24, 2013 (419 words)

It's Memorial Day weekend, which means its time to plan your summer reading. Here are three technology-related books that I recommend.

The first book is "Steve Jobs" by Walter Isaacson (Simon & Schuster, 2011). This book came out in October 2011 and I'm ashamed to say that its been sitting on my shelf ever since. My only excuse is that the book is too large to carry around (it's over 600 pages long), but there's a Kindle edition out now that solves this problem.

Enough time has passed since Jobs' death that his long-term vision for the future of Apple is only now beginning to unfold, with tantalizing hints of an Apple TV device and other developments still in the pipeline. The book is a collection of interviews with Jobs on a wide variety of topics, including his seminal role at Apple, but also touching on his time at NeXT and Pixar. He was a transformational figure in the technology world, and for that reason alone his story warrants telling.

The second book is "The New Digital Age: Reshaping the Future of People, Nations and Business" by Eric Schmidt and Jared Cohen (Knopf, 2013). This book just came out last month. The authors are both affiliated with Google: Schmidt served as CEO from 2001-2011 and Cohen is the director of Google Ideas. Schmidt was in the news recently with his much-publicized trip to North Korea, which I think reflects his growing interest in the role of technology in American foreign policy. Cohen has a longer record in this area, having served as advisor to several Secretaries of State.

Their book discusses the role of technology in the society of the near future. The authors laud the beneficial aspects of a connected world and the many advantages it offers the developing world. But they also warn of the dangers that ubiquitous surveillance by governments can pose to an unknowing population. The reviews for the book are mixed, but there's little doubt that the authors are writing about a very important topic that deserves wider discussion.

The third book is "Abundance: The Future Is Better Than You Think" by Peter Diamandis and Steven Kotler (Free Press, 2012). The book is a welcome respite from the constant negativity that fills the news. The authors argue that technology, and the innovative people behind exciting new ideas that have yet to come to market, offer solutions to many of our current problems, including fresh water, clean air, and employment opportunities. Let's hope they're right.

INFRASTRUCTURE

Let's hope the "fire sale" scenario never becomes reality

Published as "Infrastructure vulnerable to computer glitches"

May 31, 2013 (418 words)

MONTREAL – 1.3 million people ride the subway ("Metro") here everyday. Seven times in the last year the subway system has ground to a halt, causing widespread confusion. Customers are becoming increasingly exasperated at having their daily commute interrupted. Little information is provided to them for the outages. Usually they are forced to scramble to find alternate means of transportation during rush hour – not a pleasant experience when the weather outside is worse than at the North Pole.

The official reason for the repeated system failures is – you guessed it – a "computer glitch". It seems a malfunctioning computer control system doesn't like the software patches that have been applied to it over the last 11 months as part of a $200 million upgrade program. Meaningless phrases like "bad server data" and "memory saturation" are trotted out to cover the true nature of these computer glitches: poor engineering and a complicated legacy system that no one truly understands.

The latest subway shutdown took place last Tuesday. The very next day the Island of Montreal issued a "boil water" order for 1.3 of its 1.8 million residents. The water coming out of the taps was brown and murky. Officials were concerned about contamination. The cause was a malfunctioning water filtration plant nearly 100 years old. Water levels had been drained too low in the main tanks, causing sediment to mix with the drinking water before it was pumped into the pipes. The mistake appears to be human error. Like the software controlling the subway system, the filtration plant was undergoing maintenance at the time of the failure.

The subway system and the water system are just two examples of the fragile infrastructure so common to our aging cities. Both resemble a brittle and sclerotic nervous system, slowly falling into disrepair. Attempts to affect a cure often make things worse, since the physicians (engineers in this case) don't truly understand the physiology of their patient. Even the anatomy – the structure of the tunnels and pipes – is not fully known.

As computers become more and more intertwined in the essential infrastructure of modern society, problems like these will become more prevalent. It's bad enough that routine maintenance and software upgrades cause unforeseen negative consequences that so far are mostly irritants. The real worry is if someone is able to gain control of computers that control these critical systems through a cyber attack – the "fire sale" scenario in the movie "Live Free or Die Hard". Then the outcome could be far worse and more widespread.

HEAT

Personal technology can help cool you down in the summer

Published as "Personal technology to cool you down"

June 7, 2013 (416 words)

PHOENIX, Ariz. – I landed at Sky Harbor Airport late Saturday night. It was still 100°F outside. It feels odd to have warm air blowing on you when it's dark out. Our bodies are programmed to associate heat with daytime and sunlight. But here in the desert, it's hot all the time. Technically there's still two weeks of spring left before summer starts and the mercury really starts to rise.

I left Florida at the start of the rainy season. The temperatures are climbing there too, but so is the humidity. The options to stay cool in the tropical climate are rather limited: stay in the air conditioning, or embrace the daily deluge.

Here in Arizona the chances of rainfall are very small, at least until the monsoon season begins in August. So keeping cool really means staying in air conditioning, or taking precautions when outside. Besides the obvious ones, such as wearing cotton clothes and a hat, there are personal technology devices that can help keep you cool.

The simplest devices are those little handheld fans you can find in the checkout lanes. Even better are baseball hats with the fans mounted in the visors. But these are amateurish solutions. What you need is a personal cooling device.

Several years ago I bought a "Coolware Personal Cooling System" from Sharper Image. Its open donut shape makes the device look like the crashed alien spacecraft in "Prometheus." It's made of plastic and aluminum. It's filled with water and has a two-speed fan. You wear the device on your neck and it cools your entire body rather like a portable evaporative cooler. Think of how good it feels when you put a cold cloth on the back of your neck when you're hot, then imagine this feeling all the time when you wear this device.

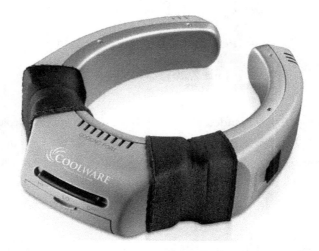

When I lived in California I wore it while installing a cat door in my garage. It was 112°F outside but I was able to do the work without being too uncomfortable. The only downside is that you look like a total dork. My friend laughed her head off at me. But she was sweating and I wasn't.

Today's forecast is intense sunshine and 111°F. So if you see a slightly geeky looking guy walking down a Valley street, it's probably me. I may look like I'm wearing a futuristic dog collar, but at least I'll feel cool. I'm no slave to fashion when it comes to comfort.

I wonder if they sell ice-lined Crocs?

PRIVACY AND SECURITY

It turns out the tinfoil hat brigade was right

Published as "Maybe the tinfoil hat brigade was right"

June 14, 2013 (418 words)

PHOENIX, Ariz. – Bluffdale, Utah is about 650 miles north of where I am in Phoenix. Both cities are situated in the middle of a desert. Bluffdale has one important difference though: it's the new home of the NSA's spy center, where some of the data vacuuming and traffic analysis is done as part of the agency's now-public surveillance program called Prism.

In the old days, wiretaps were placed on suspects' telephone lines when probable cause existed. These days, the NSA has the capability to scoop up just about every bit of information in the country (and beyond), whether it's on a wire or in the air, pretty much all the time. We're talking yottabytes ($10^{\wedge}24$ bytes, or 1 trillion terabytes) of data and powerful supercomputers crunching away to make sense of it all. It turns out the tinfoil hat brigade was right: the government really is listening.

Privacy is dead. This is the new normal. Taps are reported to be in place on the servers of major companies such as Apple, Facebook, and Google. Verizon is on record as having handed over the phone records for millions of its customers. One can only smirk when hearing the government acknowledge that the NSA is tracking call patterns, email traffic, website visits, and so on … but they're not listening to the content of the calls. Um hum. And the cheque is in the mail.

Since Internet traffic is international, the reach of the NSA program is not limited to just the US. For example, the majority of Canadian Internet data goes through US servers. And the UK's GCHQ has said it works closely with the NSA.

The whole situation is rife with irony. The same week that a 29-year old Booz Allen consultant Edward Snowden went public with details of Prism, the President was meeting with the Chinese President Xi Jinping in California. I can easily imagine a conversation like the following taking place:

President Obama: Mr. Xi, the Unites States has some concerns about the Chinese cyber-security situation.

President Xi: I agree. We thought our Great Firewall was a technical marvel, but your Prism system puts it to shame. Can you share details on how you are able to watch over all your people in such an efficient manner? We could learn from you.

The final irony is that Snowden was temporarily holed up in a hotel in Hong Kong. Perhaps he should check his map next time. He sought to evade the men in black by escaping to China?

MICROSOFT STORES

Imitation is the sincerest form of flattery

Published as "Look in the window, it's no Apple store"

June 21, 2013 (417 words)

PHOENIX, Ariz. – They say imitation is the sincerest form of flattery. If so, Microsoft must truly admire Apple, because the Microsoft retail stores are a virtual copy of the Apple stores, right down to their innovative name: Microsoft Store.

When I went to the Microsoft Store's main website and clicked on the link, "Your Scottsdale Store," I received an error message: "Sorry, there was a problem with your request." How prophetic. So much for shopping online with Microsoft I guess. So I drove down to the store (one of 45 in the country) to see it for myself.

The Microsoft Store is in the poshest mall in the area, Scottsdale Fashion Square. Nearby is the Montblanc store, where you can purchase a nice Meisterstück fountain pen for over $1,000. Directly across the way is the Tesla store, where you can pre-order your new Model S electric car for over $87,000. Clearly, Microsoft has a certain clientele in mind for their store – I'm just not sure it's the right one.

From the outside the Microsoft store looks nearly identical to the Apple store. Large windows offer a view into an open concept layout. You can tell you're about to enter the Microsoft store and not the Apple store because above the entrance is the Microsoft colored-square logo, not the silver Apple logo. But that's about the only difference from the outside.

Inside the store there are large wooden tables spread throughout. On each table are computers, phones, and other gadgets. All very much like the Apple store. Both places tend to feel like a techno-IKEA. Milling around the store are Microsoft representatives, looking very much like Apple store representatives, except their shirts are different colors. But the Microsoft representatives seem rather lonely.

Every Apple store I've visited is jam-packed with people. There's a certain buzz about the place, a sense of excitement. People clamor to see the latest notebook or smartphone. Even operating system upgrades create waves of interest.

In contrast, the Microsoft store felt tired. There weren't many customers, so the large room echoed a lot. It wasn't as bad as the Blackberry store I visited last year, which had only the sound of crickets emanating from it, but it certainly wasn't very lively either. It seems people just aren't that pumped up by heavy tablets with flat keys running a confusing operating system.

Recent news has Microsoft entering into discussions to buy Nokia's handset business. Hands up who wants a new Nokia phone running Windows Phone 8? Exactly.

REAL ESTATE

Technology today can help both buyers and sellers

Published as "Real estate apps help buyers and sellers"

June 28, 2013 (414 words)

PHOENIX, Ariz. – The real estate market here is heating up almost as fast as the daytime temperature in the desert. Median home prices in Phoenix are up over 20% from a year ago. The market in Florida is similar, with month-over-month gains the largest in six years. When the market is moving this fast, especially when we're still smarting from the property crash of a few years ago, what can buyers and sellers do to keep up?

Fortunately, powerful new technology can help. This is not your grandfather's real estate market. It's not even your father's real estate market. Technology has dramatically changed the real estate scene, putting unprecedented amounts of information in your hands, helping you make more informed decisions. If you've not bought or sold a home in a while, you'll be amazed at the power of the tools freely available to help you with your real estate needs.

Realtors rely on proprietary MLS (multiple listing service) programs, but a recent flurry of free websites and apps for your tablet or smartphone has opened up this treasure-trove of data to the general public. I use apps from Realtor.com, Trulia, and Zillow all the time now. They are great tools to help find property that satisfies certain criteria, particularly the real estate mantra of location, location, location. The apps use geo-location to locate properties on a map, letting you search by zip code, subdivision, and even specific streets.

The apps also give you fairly accurate estimates for likely sale price for your property and similar properties in your area. Historical sales data, tax records, and estimated mortgage payments are also shown automatically for most properties. Having this information in the palm of your hand while driving around the neighborhood is a huge help when it comes to narrowing your search for the perfect home, or for properly pricing your current home for a fast sale.

You can even use the apps as automated helpers by setting up watch lists on specific properties, or for properties that satisfy certain criteria (e.g., number of bedrooms, price range). The apps send you email with updates on a regular basis. When you see something you like, you can investigate it further yourself.

None of this technology obviates the need for a good realtor. It just means you, as buyer or seller, are much better prepared to discuss your needs with your realtor, and an educated customer is always preferable to one who is not quite sure what they want.

Douglas Englebart

He invented the mouse years before there was a PC

Published as "Englebart a true computing pioneer"

July 5, 2013 (413 words)

Douglas Englebart, the inventor of the computer mouse (among other things), passed away this week at the age of 88. He was a true pioneer of computing who had a profound influence on how we interact with technology today. It's not hyperbole to say that without his early work on human-computer interaction in the 1960s at the Stanford Research Institute (SRI), we'd not have the graphical user interfaces found on Windows and the Mac we take for granted today.

I often show software engineering students a jaw-dropping video that was recorded in 1968. The picture is in grainy black and white, but the content is amazing. In what is sometimes called "The Mother of All Demos," Englebart demonstrates several technologies that transformed the computing industry for decades to come.

In a little over 90 minutes he introduced the world to the computer mouse, hypertext (the precursor to the Web) with clickable links on a graphical display (at a time when text-oriented batch mainframes were the norm), networked computers, collaborative workspaces, video conferencing, and a chorded keyboard. If you search online you can watch the video for yourself.

To put the revolutionary nature of Englebart's 1968 demo in perspective, the first Mac to have a graphical interface with a mouse was released by Apple in 1984. The World Wide Web didn't publically appear until 1991.

Englebart called his invention the "X-Y position indicator for a display system." Not exactly the catchiest of phrases, but then again, he was a scientist and technologist, not a marketing person. He later said the word "mouse" was coined because there was a wire coming out of the end that looked like a mouse's tail. He never received any royalties for the mouse, which ironically was later licensed to Apple for $40,000, although he received several major awards, including the ACM Turing Award in 1998.

After his groundbreaking work in the 1960s, Englebart's views on the future of computing diverged from a younger generation of researchers who saw the personal computer as the way forward. Interestingly, the rise of the Web, smartphones with always-on access to virtually unlimited information, social networking, and centralized cloud computing with devices "at the edge" has vindicated Engelbart's original vision of augmenting human intellect. We've come full circle.

Englebart never became a billionaire like Steve Jobs or Bill Gates. In fact, much of their subsequent success was built upon his novel ideas. But he was there at the beginning, and he'll not be forgotten.

CHROMEBOOK

Everything is in the cloud

Published as "Give dad a simple PC he can actually use"

July 12, 2013 (409 words)

I've been using remote control technology for several years to help family and friends manage their computers from afar. These programs let you take control of distant machines using just your web browser and an Internet connection. They reduce the need for the user to deal with the complexities of security updates, driver installations, and other time-wasting activities.

The only way to completely eliminate these complexities is to change the way the computer operates. To do that requires a fundamentally different operating system, not minor variations on the usual Windows-based PC.

My father's HP notebook computer bought the farm a few months ago. It was only two years old, but it stopped working when the cooling fan failed on the motherboard, which cooked the CPU. There is no easy fix for this sort of total meltdown – certainly not something a senior citizen is going to repair by himself.

His computer was running Windows 7. All of the new computers run Windows 8 with the Metro user interface. Given his motor control constraints there was no way he was going to use a tablet or a laptop with a touch screen. Have you tried explaining to someone over the phone how to use Windows 8 with a mouse only? Good luck with that.

After looking at the computers on offer from the local stores, I chose a different option for my dad's new computer. I picked a Google Chromebook built by Samsung, a fundamentally different type of computer where all applications execute within the browser. It's the embodiment of net-centric computing, where everything is in the cloud.

My dad's needs were fairly typical for casual users. He needed to browse the web, play a few games, send and receive email, and chat online. The Chromebook gives him all of these things without the headaches of Windows. It boots in seconds. It updates itself automatically. There are no moving parts to damage. It weighs just 2.4 pounds. The battery lasts over six hours.

There are a few downsides with the Chromebook. Some programs that people are used to using are not available, such as Java and Office. For Office users, Google offers Docs online, which for many people is more than enough for occasional use.

At 11.6", the Chromebook's screen is smaller than I would like. Google does offer a larger model with a very high-resolution display, but it costs a lot more.

Did I mention the Chromebook cost just $249?

LOST IPHONE

What would you do if your digital life were lost while traveling?

Published as "How would you react to lost iPhone?"

July 19, 2013 (424 words)

LISBON, Portugal – Imagine you're traveling in a foreign country, far from home. Which would be worse: losing your wallet or losing your iPhone?

If you lose your wallet, many of your important identification cards (such as your driver's license) may be lost, but they can be replaced when you get home. Your credit cards need to be canceled right away, so that you don't end up with fraudulent transactions on your next statement. Fortunately, credit card companies provide insurance for this sort of thing, and some companies will overnight a new card to you almost anywhere in the world. Sadly, if you had cash in your wallet, that's just gone.

If you lose your iPhone, a whole new level of panic sets in. Believe me, I know. I lost my iPhone recently while traveling in Portugal. I was in Lisbon for a series of lectures. The days were very busy and I was not paying close attention to where I placed my phone all the time. For good reason actually: the phone (which is on Verizon's CDMA network) doesn't work in Europe (where GSM is the standard). I could only use apps while on a Wi-Fi network; I could not make actual phone calls.

Just minutes before my presentation I realized that I had lost my phone. One minute it was resting on the table at lunch, the next it was nowhere to be found. A jumble of worries flashed through my mind. I did not have a PIN code on the phone, so anyone could use it just by turning it on. Why no PIN? Because I hate having to enter the code each and every time I turn on the phone, which is many times a day.

All of my email was accessible, as well as my contact list. I had several financial apps on the phone, some of which save passwords, so my accounts could be easily accessed. I had visions of my bank funds being drained to some untraceable account in Lichtenstein or wherever.

My first naïve thought was to pick up the phone and call Apple, but I didn't have the phone. Plan B was to find a landline and call Apple, but landlines are nonexistent. Plus this was in Europe, where you need a calling card to call anyone. The final kicker was that everyone around me spoke Portuguese, not English, so who would I call?

Next week I'll tell you what I did to save my bacon. In the meantime, think about what you would do in similar circumstances.

FOUND iPHONE

How I learned to stop worrying and love the iCloud

Published as "All not lost when an iPhone is"

July 26, 2013 (421 words)

LISBON, Portugal – I was due to give a lecture in 45 minutes, but instead of preparing for my presentation I was panicking over what to do about my lost iPhone. How could I keep my digital life from being stolen and sold across Europe? Surely there's an app for that?

Indeed there is! Apple has an app called "Find My iPhone" that let's you locate your missing iPhone (or other Apple device) on a map. But this feature only works when the phone is on a network. My phone was not on a cellular network in Portugal due to the incompatible standards used. Moreover, this feature requires that you have turned on iCloud's "Fined My Phone" capability on your phone beforehand, and I couldn't remember if I had done so or not. (Luckily, I had.)

I borrowed a friend's computer and logged into my iCloud account. From there I used the Find My Phone application. It told me the phone was somewhere close by – which means it was on the open Wi-Fi network. That was the first bit of good news.

I then used the "Lost Mode" feature, which lets me remotely set a PIN code to lock the phone and display a message on the phone's screen indicating that the phone has been lost and for whoever finds it to please call me. I felt even better now that the phone was secured against unauthorized access. Just to be safe, I went online and quickly changed my banking and email passwords.

The time for my talk was rapidly approaching but there was still no news on my phone. I decided to go nuclear: I used the "Erase iPhone" feature on iCloud. This remotely wipes your phone of all personal data. It's a factory reset and the surest way to guarantee the safety of your data. But all your data is gone. It's truly a modern "salt the earth" approach to security, but it worked. I received a confirmation that the phone was now a brick.

I felt much more relaxed now, so I gave my talk as planned. After the talk was over and I was in a cheerier mood, I was putting some papers back into my knapsack when I felt the familiar contours of an iPhone, stuck under a strap at the bottom of the bag. The phone had been with me all the time. Doh!

Next week I'll tell you what I did to restore the data on my phone so that it was quickly back in working order.

Restored iPhone

What was lost was found again and now it's better than ever

Published as "Backups save recovered iPhone owner"

August 2, 2013 (423 words)

LISBON, Portugal – When I thought I had lost my iPhone while traveling in Europe, I panicked. I took the drastic step of using Apple's "Find My iPhone" service to remotely erase all the phone's data. It was secure, but it was empty.

When I found the phone, I was faced with the problem of restoring it to the way it was before. Fortunately, most of my phone's data and preferences were backed up with Apple's iCloud service. As soon as I returned to my hotel room and had access to a strong Wi-Fi signal, I began the restoration process.

I had previously set my phone to automatically maintain copies of all of my accounts, documents, and settings in the cloud. When I turned on the phone for the first time, it asked me if I wanted to restore it using a backup from my computer or a backup from my iCloud account. I chose the latter and waited for iOS to do the rest. It worked flawlessly. In a matter of minutes I had my phone working again, just as it used to be, with all of my data intact.

With one exception: my photos were not there. I had taken many pictures during my visit to Portugal and I hated the thought of losing them all. Then I remembered that I had set my iPhone to sync photos to the cloud using Photo Stream. It was a separate restoration process, but it too worked perfectly: all of my photos were copied back to my phone. Everything was back to the way it was just a few short hours ago, before the panic of losing my phone had begun.

There are a few important lessons learned from this experience. I should have set a PIN code to prevent unauthorized access to the phone, but I hate typing a 4-digit sequence every time. If the rumors are true, the next iPhone may incorporate a fingerprint scanner from Apple's acquisition of AuthenTec that would alleviate this problem. For me, this feature can't come soon enough.

I'm glad I had backups set to run automatically for data and for photos. The iCloud service really saved me a lot of time and effort. Backups are like an insurance policy: you only need them in emergencies, but when you need them you need them right away – and they better work perfectly.

Lastly, if I ever lose my iPhone again while traveling, I'll let the words from the book "The Hitch Hiker's Guide to the Galaxy" guide my actions: Don't panic.

Switching Browsers – The New Reboot

Changing browsers to run web apps is a sign of sloppy code

Published as "Switching browsers: The new reboot"

August 9, 2013 (428 words)

"Have you tried rebooting?"

How many times have we heard this lame excuse for IT support? It's the first and last thing you're told to do when speaking to customer service. It's another way of them saying, "We have no idea what's wrong, but maybe turning your computer off and then on again will magically fix the problem."

Ironically, sometimes they're right. But it doesn't make the advice any better.

These days, there's a new excuse in town. "Have you tried switching to a different browser?"

The rationale behind this advice is that different web browsers render content differently. Sadly, sometimes this is true. But it shouldn't be. Consumers should stop accepting shoddy products that don't do what they're supposed to do. Web browsers are no different.

For a long time, many websites required that you use Microsoft Internet Explorer 6 for the "best user experience". What they were really telling you is that their code had not been tested to work properly on other browsers, and furthermore, they couldn't be bothered to do so. You have to change, not them.

If you use a different platform than Windows, say Mac OS X, running old versions of Internet Explorer is not an option. The program is gone.

If you use a different browser, say Apple's Safari, Mozilla's Firefox, or Google's Chrome, you're out of luck.

I thought this was a problem of the past, until very recently when a new version of real estate software I use was released. It only works well on Firefox. For those folks who use a Google Chromebook, which only has a Chrome browser, the program is unusable.

It shouldn't be this way. The reasons are varied, but they only matter to the programmers who build the browsers and the web applications. Different versions of HTML, bugs in the rendering engine, plugins that corrupt other programs, all can contribute to the problem. To the average user, these technical reasons should be irrelevant.

To me, this is a sign of the sloppiness that has crept into software engineering. Programs are barely designed with the end user in mind. They are coded with little thought to bugs, security, or maintenance. Testing (if done at all) is rushed and perfunctory. The most important thing to do is ship the product as soon as possible.

Consumers, rise up! Vote with your wallets and send a message. Stop using crappy software – even if it's free. Channel Network's Howard Beale and shout out of your window, "I'm as mad as hell, and I'm not going to take this anymore!"

LIVESCRIBE

Digital technology comes to the written word

Published as "Digital pen a new spin on note-taking"

August 16, 2013 (413 words)

It's back to school time. Many students will be shopping for new computers. I'd like to suggest a digital twist on an old technology: the Livescribe Smartpen.

The Smartpen is basically a computer that comes in the shape of a pen. It has a tiny OLED display, a microphone and speaker, and special software built into the device. The pen itself writes normally, but when used with Livescribe's special paper, everything you write is recorded. The paper is full of tiny dots that are invisible to the naked eye, but they act as a grid for the pen's tracking software, so that it knows where on the page you are writing, and in what order.

When you use the audio recording feature, the audio is synced with your writing. If you are listening to a lecture and making notes at the same time, later you can jump to any point in the presentation simply by touching the pen to your notes.

Since you're writing with a pen on paper, you can draw figures, make parenthetical notes, and even scribble in the margins. All the text is captured by the Smartpen and later transferred to your computer to be converted into a "pencast". This is a searchable digital representation of your written notes and audio recordings. The text can be converted to Word (using a separate app) or shared with friends as interactive PDFs through email, Google Docs, or Facebook.

I think the Livescribe system is a fascinating twist on the ancient act of note taking. Most new developments are for the computer: you type on a keyboard into a special note-taking program. Or you tap words into a special app on a tablet or smartphone. Livescribe builds upon the most natural methods of note taking: writing. It enhances what we know, rather than forcing us to adopt a new technique.

I have an extensive set of acronyms and phrases that I use as index terms. I write these terms in the left margin of my notebook, so that later I can quickly scan the pages to locate notes related to particular topics. Livescribe lets me keep using this method, but makes it even better because the notebook is digitized and therefore quickly searchable across many pages.

The one drawback to Livescribe is that you must like to write your notes by hand, with a pen on paper. Old school. Sadly, cursive writing and taking notes in class both seem to be dying arts.

KNOCK THREE TIMES

It takes perseverance to get people to answer these days

Published as "'Knock Three Times' to get people's attention"

August 23, 2013 (419 words)

My life has begun to resemble the 1970 song "Knock Three Times" by Tony Orlando and Dawn. The song's lyrics tell the story of a man in love with a woman who lives in the apartment directly below his. To gauge her interest, he tells her to, "knock three times on the ceiling if you want me / twice on the pipe if the answer is no."

I've found that to gauge someone's interest in anything these days, you need to (virtually) knock on his or her door three times. We've become so inured to digital disruptions that many people have chosen to ignore the first two attempts to communicate. They expect you to keep trying and trying before they'll respond. It's annoying but it's the new reality.

It's true that there are still people of a certain age who jump up to answer the phone when it rings, no matter what they're doing. "It might be someone important," is the usual explanation. The fact that they have an answering machine seems irrelevant, since their friends "don't like to leave messages."

For the younger generation, telephone calls are quaint artifacts of the past. They don't call, and they don't do email much anymore either. They text. To reach them you need to knock three times before you get their attention.

The first knock is sending them email, where you carefully describe the situation and ask specific questions. You take time to craft a detailed note. They won't read it; anything longer than a tweet is too long to fit on a single screen, so they'll ignore the rest of the message. They probably won't reply, but if they do, it's with non-sequiturs and partial answers, pecked out on their smartphone keyboard.

The second knock is calling them on their smartphone. It rings forever and then hangs up, or it goes directly to voicemail. They never answer right away. You leave a message, but it's irrelevant, because they won't listen to it anyway. And they won't call back.

The third knock is a text message. You briefly tell them that you left them a voice mail and an email, and hope they reply. If you're lucky, they will, maybe with a simple "k". You're left wondering what that means and when a more detailed reply will follow.

Maybe you could poke them on Facebook. Or send them a Vine short video. Personally, I'm thinking old school: speak to them in person and listen for the three knocks on your ceiling.

LABOR DAY

Wasting time laboring to get technology to work

Published as "Are you addicted to technology?"

August 30, 2013 (431 words)

Does technology serve us, or do we serve technology? Does it save us time and labor everyday, or do we waste for time laboring to get technology to work?

Is technology an aid or an addiction?

To answer this question, researchers in Japan are opening "Internet fasting camps" to help the more than half a million Japanese children between 12 and 18 who are addicted to the web and related technologies. The children will spend time in controlled environments devoid of network connections, smartphones, and other computing devices.

Here at home, there have been numerous stories of summer camps that disallow all forms of computing technology. The camp counselors were finding that the kids were spending all their time indoors, texting or checking Facebook, instead of enjoying the great outdoors. Summer camp creates lasting memories of new friends, time spend around the bonfire roasting marshmallows, and having fun hiking and swimming. For many kids thee days, unplugging from their phones or tablets to experience summer camp properly is akin to going cold turkey for a drug addict.

Working adults suffer even more from technology addiction. There's a reason the BlackBerry is colloquially known as the CrackBerry: the business people who use it become dependent on it. They say they can't function anymore without it.

Ask yourself how many times you check email every day. Do you bring your smartphone to the bathroom? Do you wake up at night and send text messages? If you answered "yes" to these questions, are these not the signs of an addiction?

If you really want to see if you're addicted, visit http://netaddiction.com/internet-addiction-test/ and take the online quiz. The results can be quite startling.

It wasn't that long ago that we didn't carry computers in our pockets. Think back to that time in your life. Were you less stressed or more stressed? More productive or less productive? Were your personal relationships healthier and happier?

This Labor Day weekend, take some time away from technology. Try going cold turkey yourself, at least for one full day. Unplug. If you find yourself "jonesing" for a quick taste, maybe just to quickly check your friend's Twitter feed, take a step back and think about what's happening. Technology is the master and you're the slave.

Get your life back. Technology should be a labor saver, not a time sink. You don't need to become a Luddite and live off the grid all the time. Just become a prudent user of technology, recognizing when it helps and when it hinders.

Hopefully I'll see you at the beach this weekend. Sans smartphone.

MEMO TO MICROSOFT

Go all-in with a Skype phone

Published as "Now is the time for boldness from Microsoft"

September 6, 2013 (418 words)

Dear Microsoft,

Steve Ballmer's announcement that he's stepping down as CEO in the coming year is a wonderful opportunity to take a step back and think about the nature of your business, both current and future. There are a great many things I could suggest the company do, such as splitting Windows into truly separate PC and tablet products, or buying parts of Blackberry at a deep discount to gain access to their enterprise messaging system. But I'll recommend just one thing to do: go all-in with a Skype phone.

You bought Skype in May 20011 for $8.5 billion. Since then it's languished on the Microsoft shelf. There's a huge amount of untapped potential in the Skype brand. It could be developed into a complete platform, like Google Glass, if you only thought about the phones of the future, not the phones of the past.

Buying Nokia's handset business for $7.2 billion might pan out. Or it might fall flat. It depends on how you position the handset in the consumer space. If you continue to focus on Windows Phone as the brand, it will go nowhere. But if you use Nokia's hardware as the platform for a Skype phone, it will take off.

The phones of the future won't rely on expensive cellular data plans. They'll use Wi-Fi almost all the time. For the millions of potential customers in the developing world, a Skype phone backed by Microsoft and Nokia would be awesome.

When I travel internationally, I rarely worry about roaming rates because I don't use the cellular networks. I use Wi-Fi wherever I go. I don't make telephone calls back home. I use text messages or I use Apple's

Facetime to have video chats for no charge.

If a Skype phone could offer the same experience, it would be a game-changer. But it has to be dead simple to use. Ditch Metro's confusing tile interface and provide a more limited but more useful set of apps, with video calls using Skype being front and center. When there's no Wi-Fi around, use pay-as-you-go cell plans and the SkypeOut functionality as a backup. But over time, this option will be used less and less. Build the Skype phone assuming Wi-Fi will be free and ubiquitous.

Otherwise, you'll find yourself competing at the top end with Apple iOS (and losing on design), and competing at the bottom end with Google Android (and losing on cost). Instead, get back out front and lead through innovation. Get your mojo back.

WILL I BUY AN iPHONE 5S?

An underwhelming product refresh makes me wonder

Published as "Apple's refreshed iPhone inspires yawns"

September 13, 2013 (419 words)

This week's announcement by Apple of its new iPhones was underwhelming. With one major exception, and a few minor ones, there was nothing new. Even the screen size remained the same.

The major exception was the inclusion of a fingerprint scanner on the home button. Apple calls it "Touch ID". It uses technology they acquired from Authentec a few years ago. If it works, it will allow you to access your phone just by placing your finger on the built-in scanner; no more need to enter a 4-digit PIN code. Given the problems I had this past summer when I lost my iPhone while traveling in Europe, I think Touch ID is a great idea. I'm just a bit skeptical that it will work properly all the time, but I'll reserve my final judgment until I've had a chance to actually use the device. For now, this single feature sets the iPhone 5S apart from the competition.

The few other minor items introduced with the iPhone 5S include a faster main processor called the A7, a new co-processor called the M7, a 64-bit architecture, new photo features, and the iOS 7 operating system. From a consumer point of view, most of these are irrelevant, with the possible exception of new photo features. The A7 processor will make the phone faster, but we expect that. The M7 processor will handle gyroscopic movement, which may be useful to health and fitness apps. The 64-bit architecture is only of interest to geeks. iOS 7 will be available for Apple's other devices too, not just the iPhone 5S; you can experience it on your current phone or tablet starting September 18.

I took an informal poll among my students, asking them if they would buy an iPhone 5S. One student said "yes", but only because his contract was up and he was due for a new phone. Everyone else said "no". Most thought the upgrades were unimportant. Interestingly, the students didn't seem to care about the fingerprint scanner. This does not bode well for Apple.

As for the iPhone 5C, the students just laughed. Some said the 'C' stood for 'color', others said it stood for 'cheap', and others said it stood for something I won't repeat here. The students' response to the 5C was that if price is an issue, they'll buy an Android phone. And if they want color, they already have color cases, so why buy another?

Listen up Apple. Your user base is telling you something, loud and clear.

iOS 7

Initial impressions on Apple's new iPhone operating system

Published as "Apple's iOS 7 works great, looks so-so"

September 20, 2013 (420 words)

I've only been using it for about 12 hours, but so far my initial impression of iOS 7 from Apple is that it is a very solid software upgrade for the iPhone.

The update itself went flawlessly. The second time. The first time I tried, the phone told me I didn't have enough space left on the device. I removed some videos and restarted the process.

When the phone rebooted, the new interface was glaring me in the face. And I do mean glaring. Ugh – those icons! They are so blotchy that they look like they were ripped from an episode of "South Park". What was Johhny Ive thinking when he decided to go with fluorescent art deco colors?

And what's what those fonts? There's minimalist and then there's anorexic. I find it hard to read the clock on the front of the phone because the font is so light and so skinny. It looks more like an etching. For a company that prides itself on user interface design, I find these changes perplexing.

However, issues with icons and fonts notwithstanding, most of the other changes in iOS 7 are quite welcome. For example, I'm a bit of a weather junkie. The new weather app displays the current temperature, forecast for the day, and for the next five days. It also uses new animations, such as clouds that move slowly across the sky if it's cloudy outside. It's a subtle but nice touch.

In fact, the current weather is also reflected on the main screen of the phone, I just didn't realize it at first. I wondered why there were water droplets that moved a bit when I tilted the phone. Only when the image changed to a night sky did I realize that the phone was using the current weather and time to change the display. Duh.

There are some welcome changes to the phone and message apps that make life easier. For instance, if you're in a meeting and someone calls, there are now several default text messages that can be sent with the touch of a button, such as "Can't talk right now… I'll call you later." It's a small change, but it sure comes in handy a lot.

I've also been using iTunes Radio, which is a new streaming music service. It's much like Pandora, where you can create stations based on bands or musical genres. It works great.

iOS 7 is a free upgrade suitable for the iPhone 4 and above. Give it a try.

WIRELESS POWER

Get rid of power bars, brick-like transformers, and plug adapters

Published as "Power without cables? It could happen"

September 27, 2013 (432 words)

Do you still use an Ethernet cable to plug your computer into a network? Nowadays most people use Wi-Fi wireless networks to go online. It's the same for telephones: very few people still use a landline; more and more people use cellular only.

So why do we keep plugging our devices into the wall to get power? It's terribly archaic. I hate lugging power bars, brick-like transformers, and awkward plug adapters with me when I travel. In some cases the power supply is larger than the svelte computers they power.

Batteries are the Achilles Heel of modern computing. They never seem to last long enough. The new MacBook Air can get nearly 11 hours of continuous use on a fully charged battery. This is due to great engineering design and the use of low-voltage processors that sip the juice very slowly. But eventually the tiny batteries drain out, and we have to bring out the clumsy power brick to plug into the wall yet again.

Batteries are one of the main reasons electric cars have not taken off. To provide enough power for a typical sedan, the heavy lithium-ion battery pack takes up a huge part of the car's underbelly. And it takes many hours to recharge. Tesla is beginning to address this with supercharger stations at various locations around the country, but the fundamental problem of "plugging in" remains.

A couple of years ago I saw prototypes of charging mats. These look like hotplates and plug into a wall socket. To charge a device, like your smartphone, you place the phone on the mat. Induction coils in the mat provide power to the phone. But not all devices can be charged this way, and you still need a mat around when your batteries run low.

Why don't we just beam the power to our devices, like we beam the Wi-Fi signal? No wires, no messy connections, no worries. This is something I discussed with a friend many years ago. Obviously there are technical challenges. For example, you don't want to become the equivalent of a Hot Pocket in a microwave and have the energy zap your body as it travels from the source to any devices that need the power.

Where there's a will, there's a way. I recently saw a demo of a wireless power system called Cota from a startup called Ossia at TechCrunch's "Distrupt SF 2013" event. Cota can "charge your devices wirelessly, automatically, and safely from up to 30ft away, even through walls." The demo looked like a beta product, but it will improve.

That's true innovation.

STOP

Aargh! How do you kill this darn thing?

Published as "Stopping a wayward program not so easy"

October 4, 2013 (423 words)

In my early days of computing I was used to hitting "Ctrl-C" to stop a runaway program on UNIX. I don't know why this particular keystroke combination became the kill switch, but it always worked. If needed, you could end a program remotely using "signals" and even more arcane command sequences, such as "sudo kill -9".

When I started using an IBM mainframe operating system called VM/CMS in the late 80s, I was frustrated that there was no easy way to stop a program. Bashing away at the keyboard didn't do anything – other than make me feel better sometimes.

Fast-forward 25 years and it's back to the future. Have you ever tried to kill a program that becomes unresponsive? To put it mildly, it's frustrating. Usually, I put it more strongly while yelling at the stupid machine.

The "spinning beach ball" on the Mac has become my bugaboo. There simply is no good reason anymore for a program to get so far into the tall grass that you can't call it back. When I want a program to stop, I want it to stop. Immediately.

As a computer scientist, I understand what is going on beneath the covers. I know the nature of the operating system's scheduling program and other components of the system's runtime infrastructure. But that doesn't make the experience any better. As a user, I don't care.

I know you can (usually) go to the Finder and use the "Force Quit" option. (Assuming the program that's gone crazy isn't the Finder itself.) But I shouldn't have to do that. Simply clicking on the close ('X') button should do the trick. More often than not, clicking does nothing. And for the average user there's almost no visibility into what's actually going on. It's unacceptable that modern operating systems let programs go wild like this.

Windows users have a similar problem. There is a Task Manager program that can be used to stop errant processes, but it has an interface only a geek could love. Good luck getting grandma to understand what a "Process ID" is when all she wants to do is get Word to start working again.

When I turn off my TV or my car or the toaster, it just shuts off. It doesn't "think about it." It doesn't give me status messages to indicate where it is in the shutdown process. If I pull the plug, it stops. That's the way computers should be too.

Don't even get me started on how long it takes computers to start.

NATIONAL NEWSPAPER WEEK

Technology used to produce technology news

Published as "A salute to National Newspaper Week"

October 11, 2013 (424 words)

This is National Newspaper Week. Newspapers have always been an important part of my life. In the days before easy access to the Internet, I went to the public library and spend hours flipping through the international newspapers. I loved to read what was happening in far-away places like Australia or Scotland. Newspapers gave me an armchair traveler's view of recent events in these foreign lands.

When you think about it, the technology needed to produce a daily newspaper is quite amazing. Think of the supply chain, the workflow, and the personnel. It's like a vastly complicated machine, a mixture of analog gears and digital switches, all running constantly and set to '11', consuming data from multiple sources for rapid analysis, commentary, and reporting.

There used to be a quotidian cycle to the business, but cable news networks changed that to a 24/7/365 model. There is still a noticeable refresh period when new articles are made available (usually overnight), but breaking events are now reported as they happen using the Internet.

Each morning I pickup my printed newspaper that's been delivered overnight to my front door, and each morning I'm in awe of the work that goes into producing it. Having been a contributor for a while now, the wonder has only increased. It's like the newspaper is running a perpetual marathon, and when it finished one race, the next one starts up again right away.

Digital media has created new opportunities for the newspaper business, but it's also created more work as well. It was already challenging getting the printed edition done every day. Now there's the website that needs to be updated with content all day, videos produced and uploaded, and material synchronized across multiple platforms.

Social media is now a common part of a newspaper's output stream. Tweets, Facebook updates, and interactive forums all require nearly constant attention. They are another source of late-breaking information and can be used as community building tools quite effectively.

Tablets and smartphones are the latest addition to the devices newspapers must support. Each has a separate app that must be developed and maintained. Each has specialized technology and business models that must be managed. This is like the Wild West of publishing, and the rules are changing all the time.

Some people think daily newspapers are a thing of the past. I disagree. When I see smart and successful entrepreneurs like Jeff Bezos investing in the newspaper business, I'm reminded of a quote by Mark Twain: "The reports of my death have been greatly exaggerated."

NOBEL PRIZE IN PHYSICS

What gives matter mass is a heavy question

Published as "Nobel winners helped explain universe"

October 18, 2013 (418 words)

Theoretical physicists are deep thinkers who ask heavy questions that focus on the essence of the nature of the universe itself. In 1964, two such physicists asked, "What makes things heavy?" Actually, they didn't ask that exact question, but it's easier to understand than the question they really asked, which was, "What are the origins of mass in subatomic particles?"

The two physicists asking this question were François Englert, an emeritus professor at the Université Libre de Bruxelles in Belgium, and Peter Higgs, an emeritus professor at the University of Edinburgh in the UK. They answered this question with a theoretical framework that relied on a new particle, now called the Higgs boson, that gives other particles mass as they interact with an invisible field. Think of the field as molasses: some particles get stuck more than others as they move through it, and the stickiness is an indication of the particle's mass.

The Higg's boson went undetected for 48 years, until it's existence was confirmed through experiments at CERN in Europe last year. These experiments involve proton-proton collisions at extremely high energy, and detecting the particle is very complicated. Thousands of people are involved. The technology needed to run the experiment is nothing short of mind boggling. There is probably more computing power at CERN than anywhere else on Earth, with the possible exception of the NSA.

The Higg's boson is sometimes referred to as the "God particle" because of its role in providing order to the chaos of the cosmic soup that resulted from the Big Bang. Without the Higg's boson, particles would have no mass and therefore everything would be flying away at the speed of light and nothing would bind together to form the building blocks of life.

It sometimes takes a while for a scientist's accomplishments to be acknowledged (both Englert and Higgs are now in their 80s), but they were finally rewarded for their seminal work nearly half a century ago by winning the 2013 Nobel Prize in Physics. They will share the $1.25 million cash award. For Higgs in particular, it is formal recognition of his already popular status. It's not very often you have a subatomic particle named after yourself.

The discovery of the Higgs boson somewhat completes the Standard Model of particle physics, but it certainly doesn't mean we're all done. Dark matter, dark energy, and quantum phenomena are examples of topics that are still largely unexplained. There are still plenty of heavy questions to ask – and to answer.

FREE OS X

Apple's latest operating system given away for free

Published as "Apple's free release is no Maverick move"

October 25, 2013 (422 words)

How do you compete with free?

Apple's latest operating system for the Mac, called OS X Mavericks, is being given away for free. You can download it today from the iTunes App store. Past releases of OS X were not expensive (e.g., $19.99 for last summer's "Mountain Lion" version 10.8), but free is something else entirely.

Apple's spate of product announcements this week included the reasoning behind the giveaway: they want to get Mavericks into the hands of as many people as possible as quickly as possible. It's actually in their own interest to do so, since it saves them money in the long run by not having to maintain and support past versions of the OS for too long. And there's no better way to entice people to upgrade than to give it away.

Microsoft's flagship operating system also went through a recent upgrade, to version 8.1. For Windows 8 users, the incremental upgrade is free. For everyone else, Microsoft's own website lists the estimated retail price of Windows 8.1 at $119.99, and the Pro version at $199.99. That's a far cry from free.

When Microsoft gave away Internet Explorer for free, they were slapped with anti-trust violations and were forced to spend considerable resources defending their business practices. Competitors complained that they could not make any money when Microsoft was offering nearly the same product as they were (a web browser), but for free. Now here was are, several years later, and the tables have turned. I think it's the app ecosystem that has been the force behind the changes.

Microsoft has two flagship products: Windows and Office. Each enjoys a significant market share, so there's little chance they're going away anytime soon. In fact, *The Verge* reported that for the fourth quarter of 2013, "Microsoft's Windows division posted revenue of $4.4 billion, a six percent increase from the same period last year." But that was before their main competitor started offering their products for free.

You see, it isn't just OS X Mavericks that Apple is giving away. They are also giving away their iWork and iLife product suites for free now too. All are available as free apps on the iTunes store today. In my opinion, Mavericks is a superior operating system to Windows 8.1. But the Apple iWork suite is not as good as Microsoft Office in terms of functionality and capabilities. I still find Office annoyingly buggy, but Word offers much more than Pages for working on complex documents, so I'm stuck with it – for now.

HEALTHCARE.GOV

A scary prospect just in time for Halloween

Published as "Bungled launch of ACA website is no surprise"

November 1, 2013 (427 words)

Just in time for Halloween comes something so scary you want to run screaming into the night. An ominous phrase so full of foreboding that you know something bad will happen. It's enough to send chills down your spine.

"We're from the government and we're here to help."

This month's sad display of government technical ineptitude with the rollout of the HealthCare.gov website should come as a surprise to no one. Our elected and appointed officials have a long history of botched IT projects stretching back decades, and it seems it never gets any better.

Just before I joined Carnegie Mellon University's Software Engineering Institute (SEI) in 1995, colleagues from the SEI and MIT were asked to perform an assessment of the FAA's floundering upgrade program. It was years late and billions of tax dollars over budget. Lessons learned from this fiasco were well documented and widely publicized, but apparently never reached Washington.

The literature is full of similar doomed efforts, such as the Denver airport baggage handling system and the FBI's Virtual Case File project. Failures at this scale are one of the reasons the SEI created the Capability Maturity Model (CMM): to help determine a contractor's ability to deliver the software they promised, on time and on budget.

Fast-forward nearly 20 years and we have the world's superpower demonstrating an inability to just get a website up and running properly. It's so bad that *Saturday Night Live* opened their show last week with a masterful skit featuring Health and Human Services Secretary Kathleen Sebelius apologizing for the website and offering "helpful hints" to get around the bugs. Such as, "Have you tried restarting your computer?"

The skit ended with an offer from the government to send you a copy of "Encarta '95" and a disc from AOL to help you get online using a dialup modem. It cracked me up because it's so close to the truth.

The government's official response to the Affordable Care Act website's ills was to institute a "tech surge." I'm sure the uninformed thinking was that if it worked in Iraq, it should work online too. Sadly, the opposite is true, and it's been known for nearly 30 years. In 1975, Fred Brooks published his seminal book called *The Mythical Man-Month*, which contained many principles of software engineering gleaned from his own extensive experiences in the field. One such principle was, "adding manpower to a late software project makes it later."

It's too bad Three Stooges Development LLC, or whoever else was responsible for the HealthCare.gov website, hadn't read it.

THE REAL PROBLEM WITH VIRTUAL
MACHINES

They are good in theory but cumbersome in practice

Published as "Virtual machines offer real benefits, some difficulties"

November 8, 2013 (426 words)

A virtual machine is a software program that lets you run an operating system ("guest") on top of another operating system ("host"). Virtual machines are useful because they let you use programs not available on your host platform without purchasing a new computer. The guest operating system appears on your screen in a window just like any other program.

For example, using a virtual machine you can run Microsoft Windows 7 as a guest operating system on top of Apple Mac OS X. This would let you use special purpose software, such as corporate accounting applications only available on Windows, on your Mac. It's the best of both worlds.

Some software engineers use virtual machines as experimental sandboxes. They can try out new applications that might be buggy without fear of corrupting their development environment. The virtual machine stores a copy of the guest operating system as a large file, called an image, and it isolates the host operating system from any problems.

Several commercial programs that can run virtual machines on your Mac or PC. On the Mac there is Parallels, and on both platforms there is VMware, which is arguably the industry leader. There is also a free program called VirtualBox, originally from Sun and now from Oracle, which does a functional if not fancy job. Most of the commercial offerings have been recently updated to run on (or host) the latest operating system from Apple, OS X 10.9 Mavericks, and the latest operating system from Microsoft, Windows 8.1.

A drawback to using virtual machines is that they are resource hungry. You need a fairly powerful real machine to run the virtual machines without quickly exhausting the computing power available. The performance is acceptable, but sometimes there's a noticeable lag in normal operations like clicking on icons and launching applications. I even notice slight performance degradations on the real computer for some time after the virtual machines are shut down.

The main problem I have when using virtual machines are updates. I don't launch the virtual machine programs very often, and when I do it's usually to run a Windows program on my Mac. Every time I launch Windows it wants to go through a lengthy update cycle. When you use Windows everyday you might not notice this too much, but when you don't use it for months at a time, there is a slew of patches that must be downloaded and applied before you can use the program. It's become so cumbersome that I tend to avoid using the virtual machine at all.

THE DEATH OF PRIVACY

We are sleep walking into a dystopian surveillance society

Published as "Don't look now, our privacy is slowly slipping away"

November 15, 2013 (430 words)

Three hundred. That's the estimated number of times the average British citizen is caught on camera every day. It's hard to go incognito in the UK.

Lest we feel too smug here at home, note that there are an estimated 30 million surveillance cameras in the US.

We are sleep walking into a dystopian surveillance society. Like the proverbial frog slowly boiling to death in a pot of hot water, our privacy is dying little by little and for the most part, we don't seem to care.

When Samuel Warren and Louis Brandeis (a future US Supreme Court Justice) wrote their seminal paper, "The Right to Privacy" for the *Harvard Law Review* in December 1890, they were concerned with photographs taken without their permission of their private affairs being made public through publication as gossip in tabloid newspapers. I wonder what Warren and Brandeis would think of modern's society's perspectives on privacy today, nearly 120 years later? They probably would be astounded at the role of technology in influencing our views of privacy.

Nearly 15 years go, Scott McNealy, who was CEO of Sun Microsystems (now owned by Oracle) at the time, was famously quoted in *Wired* magazine as saying, "You have zero privacy anyway. Get over it." His words were prescient. Today, our privacy is being eroded by our own personal actions, by commercial companies harvesting our data to sell as a commodity, and by government programs that monitor our communications.

Do you use Google? If so, do you understand their privacy policy? It's posted online at http://www.google.com/policies/privacy/. It's a fascinating read. You'd be amazed at what Google can do with cookies –

the ones you say "yes" to all the time when using your browser. This week Google stated its intention to start using your photograph as part of its "Shared Endorsements" program in third-party ads for products and services. You agreed to this when you agreed to their terms of service.

Do you use Facebook? If so, do you understand how your online actions can affect the personal privacy and professional reputation of your online friends and family? They can become collateral damage without you even knowing about it. Facebook's privacy policy is posted online at http://www.facebook.com/about/privacy/, but most people have never bothered to read it before agreeing to it.

Do you use email or cell phones? If so, are you aware that almost all network communications are monitored by various government agencies – in particular the NSA? It gives a whole new meaning to the catch phrase, "Can you hear me now?" Today the answer is always "yes".

Quantum Computing

The biggest change in computing since vacuum tubes

Published as "Super computing takes a quantum leap"

November 22, 2013 (423 words)

The world's fastest computer is the Tiahne-2, which is at China's National University of Defense Technology. This supercomputer is powered by over 3 million Intel Xeon processors and has been clocked at 33.68 petaflops. A petaflop is a quadrillion (1,000 billion) floating point operations per second. That's really fast.

As fast as it is, there are some problems that Tiahne-2 could never solve, even if we let it run for thousands of years. That's because of the inherent limitations of the computer's digital architecture. What's coming next is a dramatically different type of computer, one that is based on the very unusual principles of quantum physics.

Quantum computers make use of entanglement to work their magic. Einstein called entanglement "spooky action at a distance." He was referring to the phenomenon of two subatomic particles sharing the same properties, even while separated by long distances.

No one really understands how entanglement really works. Various theories have been proposed, including seemingly outlandish ideas such as parallel universes, but the truth is we don't know. As one theoretical physicist recently told me, "[entanglement] just is."

Quantum computers also rely on superposition to give them their parallel processing capabilities. Traditional computers manipulate bits, which are either on ('1') or off ('0'). In a quantum computer, information is encoded in qubits, which exist in both states simultaneously.

As with entanglement, superposition is not entirely understood. It seems counterintuitive to suggest that a particle can be in more than one state at the same time. It seems even more outlandish to suggest that the particle collapses into one of its possible states simply by observing it — almost as if it was aware of being watched, but it's been experimentally shown to be true many times.

Using quantum computers, certain problems can be solved exponentially faster than with a regular computer. Problems like cryptography, which are at the heart of secret communications and credit card transactions, are currently "unbreakable" but become solvable in real time. The problems that Tiahne-2 could never solve can be solved very quickly by a quantum computer.

Building quantum computers is a devilishly hard task, but they do exist today in the lab. Fortunately, engineers don't need to fully understand the physics of the underlying principles to build machines that exploit their unique behavior. There's even a commercial company called D-Wave that sells a 512-qubit quantum computer right now. It costs over $10 million, but it's real.

Quantum computing represents the biggest change in information technology since the introduction of vacuum tubes. I call it amazing.

THANKSGIVING

Giving thanks for technology that improves our lives

Published as "Disasters remind us of what we have"

November 29, 2013 (413 words)

The widespread destruction caused by Typhoon Haiyan in the Philippines, and the devastation caused by the tornadoes that recently struck the Midwest, reminded me of the fragile nature of our technology-dependent society. It doesn't take much for us to revert to a simpler lifestyle reminiscent of the time of our Founding Fathers. We should be thankful for the more resilient technologies that enable our modern society.

We take our infrastructure for granted – until it's gone. When a winter storm hits our friends and family up north, they go from staying safe and snug in their homes to shivering in the cold waiting for the power to be restored. Here is Florida we have the opposite problem: when a hurricane knocks out the power, we all swelter in the heat and humidity. Basic things like electricity and clean water are available to us literally at the flick of a switch, but there's a lot of technology working behind to the scenes to make this possible. Candles are romantic but not very practical, and outhouses lost their appeal with bug-infested camping trips long ago.

We take transportation for granted – until we have no quick way of getting where we want to go. We hear about delays at the airport and traffic jams on the roads. These are certainly annoying, but they sure beat the alternative: no cars or airplanes. Can you imagine what it would be like without the highway system that links our cities and states together? Riding is horse is great fun, but it's sure a slow way of traveling. The 3 hours it takes to drive to Miami becomes days of meandering through swamps. We complain about jet lag and the 10 hours it takes to fly to Europe, but the alternative route of using an ocean-going ship takes much longer. And there's all that seasickness to deal with.

We take networked communications for granted – until we need to make a call in an emergency and can't find a phone. Nowadays most of us carry smartphones that let us "reach out and touch somebody" almost anywhere on the planet. The notion of long distance seems quaint to the younger generation, since they grew up in a world where cell phones and text messages have global reach – and cost almost nothing. Imagine how our daily lives would change if we all had to switch back to posting letters. Come to think of it, that might not be a bad idea for the Holidays.

SAND

Sand is used in computer microprocessors and oil fracking

Published as "Simple sand is a building block for technology's basic pieces"

December 6, 2013 (417 words)

It's not obvious that something as simple as sand plays such an important role in technology today. But it does. In fact, without sand, we'd be without the microprocessors that power our everyday computers and smartphones.

Companies like Intel that manufacture computer chips perform modern alchemy. Instead of turning lead into gold, they magically turn sand (silicon) into wafers that contain millions of transistors. They don't use the same type of sand that's found on our beaches, but the process is essentially the same. The silica is purified far beyond what's found in nature using a combination of heat and chemical treatments. The silica is spun into rods and then sliced like salami. A photo-etching process is used to imprint the circuit onto the silicon and the result is a CPU.

It's possible to use elements other than silicon to manufacture computer chips. For example, Cray experimented with the use of gallium arsenide in some of its early supercomputers. The chips run faster, but they are much more expensive and much more difficult to make. For now, silicon is the main ingredient in computer chips.

Sand is also an essential ingredient in another technical marvel: hydraulic fracturing (fracking), a new technique that is used to extract oil hidden in shale rock formations. The US is the world leader in this emerging area, and it's one of the reasons we're on track to be a net exporter of oil and gas within the next few years.

With fracking, sand is mixed with chemical and water and injected at high pressure into shale. The injection uses horizontal drilling to get to the formations. The injected mixture causes small fractures in the rock, which lets the trapped oil and gas escape. Without sand as a cheap abrasive, the process would not be possible. Companies involved in fracking in places like the Bakken Formation in North Dakota must import the sand from quarries in Wyoming and elsewhere in the Midwest.

Many places where oil is abundant (e.g., the Middle East) have few other natural resources. There's been a long-standing joke that once the oil in the ground runs out, these countries had better hope they can make a living selling sand. Turns out, they may.

It's an ironic twist of fate that the countries that had oil may run out of it, but they'll have plenty of sand, while the countries that are increasing their oil production will need sand. That's capitalism at its finest: find a need and fill it.

NEST PROTECT

A technical upgrade to the venerable smoke detector

Published as "New-age smoke detector a bit smarter"

December 13, 2013 (425 words)

I wasn't surprised when hotel security started banging on the door. Their internal alarm system had warned them of a possible fire in my unit. When they opened the door they found the place covered in smoke – and me standing in the middle of the kitchen frantically waving a dishtowel under the smoke detector. There was no fire, but there was a very burnt turkey in the oven that was giving off a lot of smoke from the hot oil in the pan. What was supposed to be a great Thanksgiving meal in a posh resort away from home turned out to be a farcical but memorable dinner experience.

With Christmas just around the corner, turkey burning may make another appearance in my household. I doubt I'll be able to improve by cooking skills by then, but I can improve the smoke detectors so that they don't go off quite so often due to minor kitchen issues. Of course the smoke detector needs to alert you when smoke is present, but you should be able to control its behavior more easily than just waiving a towel at it like a crazed matador.

Nest, the same company that brought us the digital thermostat last year, has released its next product aimed at modernizing erstwhile boring home devices: the Nest Protect. This is a combination smoke and carbon monoxide detector that is as elegant as it is functional. It's Wi-Fi enabled and controllable by a smartphone app. This means you can receive alerts remotely, no matter where you are traveling. It communicates with your Nest thermostat if you have one, for example to shut off the gas furnace if it detects real smoke in your house indicative of a possible fire.

The Nest Protect has a soothing voice that warns you if it detects anything. You can turn if off temporarily if you know you're going to be creating smoke – like burning a turkey. You can even waive your hands underneath it in a gesture rather like the dishtowel scenario to turn it off. And it acts as a nightlight with a reassuring glow near the ceiling.

At $129 the Nest Protect is not for everyone. Most people rarely think of the smoke detectors in their house until they hear that annoying beeping sound telling you to replace the batteries. But once you see a Nest Protect in action, you wonder why no one else has updated how smoke detectors work over the years. It seems obvious in hindsight, but them again, so do most true innovations.

DELIVERY

The future of package delivery is drones, robots, and printers

Published as "The sky may not be the limit in deliveries of future"

December 20, 2013 (421 words)

Hands up everyone who hasn't finished their Christmas shopping? I thought so. Me too. Every year I vow to get my shopping done early, and every year I find myself in a mad scramble to finish before the stores close on December 24.

Like many people, I've been doing an increasing amount of my shopping online. I shudder to think how much money I've donated to Amazon over the years. The Achilles Heel for online retailers has always been the "last mile": how to deliver your packages from their distribution centers to your house quickly and inexpensively.

Three recent developments have the potential to drastically disrupt the traditional package delivery system in the coming years: drones, robots, and printers.

Amazon.com Prime Air: Amazon captured everyone's attention at Thanksgiving with their announcement of *PrimeAir*, a revolutionary delivery system that uses small unmanned drones to airlift small packages right to your doorstep within 30 minutes.

I was fortunate to experience Amazon's same-day delivery service in Phoenix this summer, and the convenience of having your purchases delivered in a few hours was well worth the extra $3 fee. One can only imagine how 30-minute deliveries will change the retail landscape.

Google and Boston Dynamics: Google's purchase this week of animal-themed robotics maker Boston Dynamics is the latest sign that

Google is serious about robotics and autonomous vehicles. This is the eighth robotics company they've bought this year. Coupled with Google's driverless cars and there's a clear trend emerging, but towards what is not entirely known.

If you've seen one of the videos online of Boston Dynamics' robots navigating difficult terrain then you've seen a vision of the future. Let's hope the robots are used for useful purposes, such as delivery of emergency supplies to places humans can't go (e.g., reactor breaches), and not for more Terminator-like scenarios.

3D Printing: Drones and robots can deliver physical packages, but why bother? That's so analog. A better way might be to go totally digital and deliver only the bits needed to recreate the package. In other words, you wouldn't buy the item; you'd buy the instructions for building it. The instructions are fed to a 3D printer and voila! You have the product you ordered built immediately, in your own home. All you need is the 3D printer, which is already available.

3D printers are still somewhat limited, but technology will quickly change that. Until it's supplanted by even more revolutionary package delivery mechanisms, like quantum teleportation. But that might take a bit more time to perfect.

LOOKING BACK AT 2013

What was hot and what was not in technology in 2013

Published as "Tech issues dominated this year's news"

December 27, 2013 (426 words)

It's been a busy year for technology. I don't think a day has gone by that a leading news story didn't have some form of computerization as the culprit. I'd pick privacy, complexity, and fragility as the top three themes of 2013.

Privacy: Eye-tracking phones and Google Glass are two technologies with significant privacy implications. Google Glass, in particular, is causing both excitement and concern due to its surreptitious photographic capabilities.

But Edward Snowden is the poster child for the death of privacy. The information he's been leaking since the summer concerning the NSA's wide-reaching surveillance programs is further evidence that the government monitors everything we do.

The faux outrage expressed by foreign leaders when it was reported their cell phones were hacked and their communications recorded was amusing. The only thing they were really upset about was that it had been made public. And perhaps there was a little bit of technology envy on display as well.

It's good to know that when it comes to tech toys, we're still number one!

Complexity: The digital train wreck known as HealthCare.gov was just the latest example of the inability of lumbering organizations to design, develop, and deploy large-scale applications in a timely and cost-effective manner.

It gives me no pleasure to point out that the federal government has a history of botched projects that cost taxpayers billions of dollars. It's true that the complex legal issues underlying the Affordable Care Act are part of the problem.

But the sad fact is that the Chinese put a robotic rover on the moon last week and we're still trying to get a website working properly. Where has the can-do spirit of the Apollo days gone?

Fragility: Large cities such as Montreal have been plagued by infrastructure problems caused by computer glitches this year. Cyclones, tornados, and ice storms all have the ability to quickly knock us back to the Middle Ages due to the fragility of our technologies.

When you start using sophisticated thermostats, networked smoke detectors, and personal fitness trackers, you realize just how omnipresent technology has become in our everyday lives.

When I lost my iPhone while traveling in Portugal this summer I realized how dependent I had become on it. My email, account information, and every other app I use on a daily basis was suddenly gone. Fortunately I was able to restore the missing information fairly quickly, but I daresay it wouldn't be as easy with some of the other devices I have come to rely upon.

We need to strengthen our digital infrastructure.

ABOUT THE AUTHOR

Scott Tilley is a Professor in the Department of Education and Interdisciplinary Studies at the Florida Institute of Technology, where he is Director of Computing Education. He is Chair of the Steering Committee for the IEEE Web Systems Evolution (WSE) series of events and a Past Chair of the ACM's Special Interest Group on Design of Communication (SIGDOC). He is an ACM Distinguished  Lecturer. His current research focuses on software testing, cloud computing, educational technology, STEM outreach, and system migration. He writes the weekly "Technology Today" column for the *Florida Today* newspaper (Gannett). His recent books include *Hard Problems in Software Testing: Solutions Using Testing as a Service* (TaaS) (Morgan & Claypool, 2014) and *Testing iOS Apps with HadoopUnit: Rapid Distributed GUI Testing* (Morgan & Claypool, 2014).